Debra Allcock Tyler

2nd edition

IT'S TOUGH AT THE TOP

The No-fibbing Guide to Leadership

directory of social change

Published by the Directory of Social Change (Registered Charity no. 800517 in England and Wales)

Head office: Resource for London, 352 Holloway Rd, London N7 6PA

Northern office: Suite 103, 1 Old Hall Street, Liverpool L3 9HG

Tel: 08450 77 77 07

Visit www.dsc.org.uk to find out more about our books, subscription funding websites and training events. You can also sign up for e-newsletters so that you're always the first to hear about what's new.

The publisher welcomes suggestions and comments that will help to inform and improve future versions of this and all of our titles. Please give us your feedback by emailing publications@dsc.org.uk.

First published 2006
Reprinted 2007
Digital edition first published 2013
Second edition 2017

ISBN 978 1 78482 020 6 (print edition)
ISBN 978 1 78482 021 3 (digital edition)

British Library Cataloguing in Publication Data
A catalogue record for this book is available from the British Library

Illustrations by Grizelda
Cover and text design by Kate Griffith
Typeset by Marlinzo Services, Frome
Printed and bound by Page Bros, Norwich

Dedication

For the staff and trustees at DSC – for making it less tough
than it could be.

Contents

About the Directory of Social Change

The Directory of Social Change (DSC) has a vision of an independent voluntary sector at the heart of social change. The activities of independent charities, voluntary organisations and community groups are fundamental to achieve social change. We exist to help these organisations and the people who support them to achieve their goals.

We do this by:

- providing practical tools that organisations and activists need, including online and printed publications, training courses, and conferences on a huge range of topics;
- acting as a 'concerned citizen' in public policy debates, often on behalf of smaller charities, voluntary organisations and community groups;
- leading campaigns and stimulating debate on key policy issues that affect those groups;
- carrying out research and providing information to influence policymakers.

DSC is the leading provider of information and training for the voluntary sector and publishes an extensive range of guides and handbooks covering subjects such as fundraising, management, communication, finance and law. We have a range of subscription-based websites containing a wealth of information on funding from grant-making charities, companies and government sources. We run more than 300 training courses each year, including bespoke in-house training provided at the client's location. DSC conferences, many of which run on an annual basis, include Management Fair, the Charity Accountants' Conference and the Charity Law Conference. DSC's major annual event is Charityfair, which provides low-cost training on a wide variety of subjects.

For details of all our activities, and to order publications and book courses, go to www.dsc.org.uk, call 08450 777707 or email publications@dsc.org.uk.

About the author

Debra has been the Chief Executive of the Directory of Social Change (DSC) since 2001. She is currently a Trustee of In Kind Direct, a Patron of the Charity Staff Foundation and Vice-Chair of Governors of Whiteknights Primary School. She was a member of the Charity Commission's SORP Committee and is a Fellow of the Royal Society for the encouragement of Arts, Manufactures and Commerce (FRSA). She is also a member of the Royal Institution and Liberty. She was the founder Chair of the Small Charities Coalition.

After a brief stint in the private sector Debra has spent most of her career in the charitable sector, carrying out a range of roles at all levels, including campaigning, policy development, sales, product development, media relations and training. She spent some 14 years as a voluntary Trade Union Officer, a year working with Youth at Risk – an organisation that works to rehabilitate young people who suffer severe social disadvantages – and was the first female Programme Director of the Runge Effective Leadership programme.

Debra is an internationally published author of several books. She has spent many years working with the media, doing TV, radio, newspaper, magazine and internet features and interviews. She is a regular columnist for *Third Sector* magazine. She delivers around 50 keynote speeches every year to the voluntary, private and public sectors on topics ranging from the relationship between the state and charities to leadership and governance, and topical issues affecting the voluntary sector.

Acknowledgements

There are many people who have informed and inspired me, not least those chief execs and senior staff whom I have spent time with either through networking or training events over the last few years. I am sorry I can't name you all and forgive me if I have missed you out. There are some in particular who I would like to specifically mention.

Jeanette Allen
Deborah Annetts
Neil Betteridge
Lindsay Boswell
Caron Bradshaw
Ian Bruce
Rodney Buse
William Butler
Dr Beverley Costa
Kevin Curley
Susan Daniels
Fiona Dawe
Kathleen Duncan
Fiona Ellis
Quentin Elston

Andrew Forrest
Andy Garnett
Diana Garnham
Jane Gurney
Andrew Hind
Catherine Johnstone
Simon Kelson
Linda Laurance
Deborah Layde
Ian Lawson
Dame Suzi Leather
Archie Lightfoot
Margaret Lloyd
Ray Lock
John Low

Linda McGowan
Jan McLoughlin
Sheridan Maguire
Tony Morgan
Alistair Mortimer
Maria Pemberton
Mike Phillips
Fiona Reynolds
Pat Ryan
Frank Steer
Lesley Thornley
Peter Wanless
Jamie Wilcox

DSC is grateful to the following people and organisations for their permission to reproduce their copyright materials.

The Society of Authors, on behalf of the George Bernard Shaw Estate, for their permission to reproduce George Bernard Shaw's material.

The quote from Andrew Marr's work is reproduced with permission of Pan Macmillan via PLSclear (copyright © Andrew Marr 2004).

'The Leader' from *Sky in the Pie* by Roger McGough reprinted by permission of Peters Fraser & Dunlop (www.petersfraserdunlop.com) on behalf of Roger McGough.

John Wiley and sons Limited (Books) for their permission to reproduce a quote from Richard Hackman's (ed.) book (copyright © 1990 by Jossey-Bass).

Kriss Akabusi and the Akabusi Company for their permission to use a quote from Kriss Akabusi's work.

Extract from *The House at Pooh Corner* by A. A. Milne. Text copyright © The Trustees of the Pooh Properties 1928. Published by Egmont UK Ltd and used with permission.

Foreword

In all the sectors effective leadership matters, but especially so in the voluntary and charitable sector. When we get it wrong it's those people we are set up to serve who suffer. This is why leadership at very senior levels can be both rewarding and terrifying all at the same time, especially when you're just starting out. But really effective leadership can change the world and people's lives for the better. The NSPCC would not be as powerful a force for good in the lives of children without the ability and achievements of a succession of committed, creative and passionate chief executives creating an atmosphere where purposeful, wonderful and willing staff and volunteers focus together on how we can best improve the lives of our nation's children.

So it matters that we get it right. Of course most of us end up learning on the job, the hard way. But knowing you're not alone helps. This book is a bit like a 'pocket' mentor. You can hear Debra's voice in your ear guiding and advising with practical, sensible, no-bull**** advice. The book is littered with real-life examples of things going wrong as well as right, shared with a light and humorous touch which makes the whole business of top-level leadership seem much less tough than it sometimes feels. Go into many offices of CEOs in our sector and you will find well-thumbed copies close at hand. Its ideas have got many of us over rough ground more lightly. Perhaps it should be retitled 'In Case of Emergency Open Here'!

Enjoy the read. Apply the advice. And good luck on your leadership journey.

Peter Wanless
Chief Executive, NSPCC
Former Chief Executive, Big Lottery Fund

Foreword

Introduction

People have more need for models than critics.
Attributed to Scott Simmerman, US management
consultant

In the ten years since this book was published an enormous amount has changed in our sector and in our society. We've seen a change of government, the collapse of the banking system, a global economic crisis, a refugee and migrant crisis, a resurgence of terrorism and a couple of royal babies. But all of this upheaval has simply reinforced for me that the fundamental principles of leadership don't change regardless of the circumstances.

So the core messages in this book are largely the same. I've updated some of my stories and examples, refreshed some language but it is still filled with other people's ideas and solutions which I have 'borrowed' so I can share them with you.

The content of this book is still largely drawn from some of the most common issues and experiences in leadership that I have come across not only in my own personal experience but also working with other chief execs and senior staff in the sector. Most of my advice, hints and tips, ideas and experiences have been shared with me by hundreds of chief execs and their top teams over a number of years. The book still focuses on the more 'human' side of leadership – that is the relationships and structures that help us to persuade folk to follow us and our cause.

As always, when you read this book there will be things that you don't agree with or that don't square with your own experience. Give some of the ideas a try anyhow, and if they don't work, try something else. Working with voluntary sector organisations and their leaders has shown me that the model required depends on so many different factors – the size of the organisation, its age, its revenue, its cause and so on. And, of course, it is highly dependent on the personality, value set and background of you – the person leading the organisation. Think of leadership as a toolkit, full of different models, ideas and approaches, and take from the toolkit the tool that fits the situation you are currently in. When that situation changes, or if that particular tool didn't work, well, then you try another one.

For those of you who are already very experienced many of the ideas here may simply serve as a reminder of what you already know; for those of you who are new they may be things that you haven't tried yet. Either way leadership isn't static, situations and environments change so the tools you choose will also change, even though the fundamental principles don't.

If you're doing the job well you will probably find that you worry a lot about how you're doing! Good. Constantly thinking you could do better or try a different way is a great indication of how engaged you are in your leadership journey.

When sometimes I feel very unsure about why I am working in the charitable sector at all – or when I wonder if it's really worth the inevitable stress that comes with leading in the voluntary sector – the following quotes keep me going because they remind me of why it's worth it.

> This is the true joy in life, the being used for a purpose recognized by yourself as a mighty one; the being thoroughly worn out before you are thrown on the scrap heap; the being a force of Nature instead of a feverish selfish little clod of ailments and grievances complaining that the world will not devote itself to making you happy. ...
>
> I am of the opinion that my life belongs to the whole community and as I live it is my privilege – my *privilege* to do for it whatever I can. I want to be thoroughly used up when I die, for the harder I work, the more I love. I rejoice in life for its own sake. Life is no brief candle for me; it is a sort of splendid torch which I've got a hold of for the moment and I want to make it burn as brightly as possible before handing it on to future generations.
>
> George Bernard Shaw, Irish playwright

This next quote is the one I read during the times I feel most beleaguered; when my confidence is low, when I am wondering if we are making the right decisions at the right time, or when it really does feel as though I am swimming upstream and the tide against me is the rest of the world! (I know that some of you reading this sometimes have those feelings too – and that I am not alone in this.)

> It is not the critic who counts; not the man who points out how the strong man stumbles, or where the doer of deeds could have done them better. The credit belongs to the man who is actually in the arena, whose face is marred by dust and sweat and blood; who strives valiantly; who errs, who comes short again and again, because there is no effort without error and shortcoming; but who does actually strive to do the deeds; who knows great enthusiasms, the great devotions; who spends himself in a worthy cause; who at the best knows in the end the triumph of high achievement, and who at the worst, if he fails, at least fails while daring greatly, so that his place shall never be with those cold and timid souls who neither know victory nor defeat.
>
> Theodore Roosevelt, speech at the Sorbonne, Paris

Good luck!

1 **What they don't tell you**

*Upon his royal face there is no note
How dread an army hath enrounded him.*
William Shakespeare, *Henry V*

Outcomes
After reading this chapter you will:
- **Understand the realities of an apparently powerful job title**
- **Have a sense of the behaviours you are likely to encounter**
- **Realise the importance of critical mass**

The chances are that by the time you read this book you are already at the top or near the top of your organisation. So I'm not going to waste any time asking you whether you are sure you are ready for the challenge! But what I will say is that I believe that leadership is a vocation, not a profession.

You have probably now begun to realise that leadership is a choice you make about how to behave. The job title, 'director' or 'chief executive', does not confer automatic leadership power on you. All it gives you is a certain level of authority, but authority is not leadership. You have to make a conscious choice to engage in the leadership thinking and behaviour that turns a job title into a leadership role.

The job title is a burden more than a blessing

As soon as you gain a job title that implies status and prestige, there will be a number of people, both within and outside your organisation, who will perceive you only through the 'fog' of that job title. They will attribute to you motives that have nothing to do with who you are as a human being, and everything to do with how they perceive senior people.

I attended a do at the House of Commons several years ago. (Dos at the House of Commons are commonplace in the sector! You end up going to an awful lot of them.) I was in conversation with someone when a very senior and well-known chief executive of a large national charity came over. He clearly wanted to speak to the person who I was talking to and so simply cut in and completely ignored me. I wasn't particularly offended because this frequently happens when you are a woman leader in what is still essentially a man's world (being short and blonde doesn't help either!) and so you tend to ignore it.

Anyhow, my colleague was embarrassed by this and introduced me to this man by name and said that I worked for the Directory of Social Change (DSC).

1

He didn't recognise my name (and frankly why should he?). Looking rather irritated at having to speak to me rather than my colleague, he asked me 'Are you helping out here today?' He was clearly under the impression that I was part of the administration team. I didn't mind that either, my career began with administrative roles and I think they are massively important and underrated. So, still not being offended, I replied 'No'. To be honest, he didn't give the impression that he really wanted to talk to me so I didn't feel encouraged to open up.

My colleague then told him my job title. 'Debra is the Chief Executive.' You would be amazed at the change in his demeanour then. Suddenly I was someone of importance because I had this job title. Immediately his eyes lit up and his body language changed from dismissive to attentive. That was when I did begin to feel offended. The only thing that had influenced his desire to engage in conversation with me was when he thought of me as somebody important. As an administrator I wasn't worth the time and effort of conversation, as a chief executive I was.

This happens internally too. When I took on the leadership role at DSC my then PA, Jill Thornton, was someone who I worked alongside in a different capacity many years ago. So she knew me quite well and has seen me develop and grow over the years. When she became my PA at DSC, one of the first things she observed was that the staff found it almost impossible to see past my job title and that the person they were describing to her was not someone she recognised from her own experience.

So people will have a perception of you that is first of all based on your job title. And that perception will be highly influenced by their experiences of senior people in the past and their expectations of how you should or should not behave or act. Good leaders recognise this and take it into account when dealing with others.

You work with adults, not children: allow them to shine

One of the things I find both frustrating and amusing when observing leaders in action is how easy it is for them to forget that they employ and work with adults, not children or pupils.

We employ adults who make important decisions in their own lives, decisions that are usually more important in the wider context than those they make at work: where to live, how to educate their children, who to have relationships with, how to manage their money, who to vote for, and so on. And yet, these same people walk into work and are asked to sign a chit for a pen out of the stationery cupboard, or are not allowed to make on-the-spot decisions to help out or serve a beneficiary/service user/volunteer/customer because they have to get permission. And so often those permissions are petty, silly things that simply get in the way of getting the job done.

In your organisation everyone is important. On many days they are more important than you. In my own organisation, when we have a lot of people attending our events, the most important person is Jill Thornton (former PA, now Facilities Manager), because she has to make sure they are fed and watered and generally looked after. And she is the one who needs to make the decisions on that day about that work. She sees more of our customers than most other people in the entire organisation and she, therefore, has a bigger influence on how they perceive us and what we do than anyone else, including me.

Somehow, however, there is a two-way perception that leaders are supposed to be better, wiser, more influential and more knowledgeable than the people who they are leading. But how can they be? How can you be? The range of things that you are concerned with as you become more senior in an organisation is so wide that you cannot be expert in any of them any more. Your job is to employ the experts – and not just to advise you on what decisions you should take but to actually take the decisions about the areas in which they are expert. Your job is to surround yourself with people who know what they are doing and create an environment that helps them to shine. So many leaders behave like either teachers or parents and then get surprised and upset when their staff or volunteers behave like children or rebellious students!

The chief executive I admire the most is a guy called Tony Morgan who was one of my CEOs when I worked at the Industrial Society. He used to say that 'good leadership is about giving other people the space to show up'. In other words, letting them shine.

You need to develop a deep sense of appreciation for the efforts and aspirations of others in your organisation. The best leaders I have come across really, really do believe that they are not better than anyone else and will openly acknowledge that others are more skilled and experienced in particular areas. This is not paying lip service – it is the truth. And if it isn't the truth, if you really are appointing people into jobs that they don't do better than you, then you have to ask yourself *why* you aren't appointing more capable people.

And I do not buy the argument that says you can't get the quality of staff you need because of the relatively low levels of pay in the sector. There are a lot of skilled, intelligent, capable people out there who are not solely driven by the salary. If you don't believe your staff are high performers I suspect that you need to ask yourself if the question is not whether they have the right skills and experience but whether you're the sort of boss who can't let go. Your job as a leader is to remember that you pay them to be the expert so *you have to let go*. Be honest with yourself – is it you who is preventing them from being fabulous, even inadvertently?

You're not really human any more

The reality is that when you aspire to lead others you will largely cease to be seen as a human being with the same fears, worries, hang-ups and hopes as them. Even though you probably feel all too human and fallible, most people both want and deserve a leader who they can look up to. That doesn't mean that they will always like you. Being moaned about behind your back is actually part of the job description! But they need someone who they believe deep down, when push comes to shove, can lead the organisation in the right direction. The biggest test of your leadership ability is not what people do and say when things are going well (anyone can lead success), it's what they do and say when times are tough.

They will expect more of you in terms of how you look, what you say and how you behave. They will notice your mistakes. They will be alert for any signs of hypocrisy. They will be generally unforgiving of the times when you are, or appear to be, hypocritical or unhelpful or obstructive. And even if they forgive, they sure as anything don't forget!

Your nerves and stress levels, if seen by others, will have a disproportionate impact on the nerves and stress levels of those around you. The more worried or stressed you are, the more worried and stressed they will be. The more calm and positive you are, the more calm and positive they will be.

They have high expectations – often unreasonable in the context of you as a human being but completely reasonable in the context of you as the guardian of the organisation and, ergo, their working lives. It means the pressures on you are exceptionally high – and you need to have the strength of character to accept it and deal with it. It's part of what you're paid for.

Nobody likes you!

So you have to develop a healthy and robust sense of self. You will be criticised, sometimes fairly and sometimes unfairly, the moment you step into a senior role. And this criticism will come at you from all angles. Richard Olivier, in his excellent book, *Inspirational Leadership: Henry V and the Muse of Fire*, quotes from Shakespeare's *Henry V* where Henry is 'walking the job' (see Chapter 4) around the camp anonymously the night before the Battle of Agincourt, listening to the troops talking and complaining about him and his leadership.

In the play, Henry then gives a monologue about how hard leadership is and how often you are blamed for all sorts of things that really aren't your fault.

> Upon the king! let us our lives, our souls,
> Our debts, our careful wives,
> Our children and our sins, lay on the king!

We must bear all...
...What infinite heart's-ease
Must kings neglect, that private men enjoy!

William Shakespeare, Henry V

You will find that people around you are judging you constantly. I sometimes think that leadership is a bit like being a politician – people really don't care much about how hurtful their comments or criticisms are – it's free for all in slinging mud! And this judgement will come from trustees, staff, volunteers, partners, even beneficiaries, and of course others in the sector.

A former colleague of mine, Steve Prince, shared with me this great saying. 'Isn't it funny how we judge ourselves by our motives and others by their actions?' That pithy little phrase has always struck me as being tremendously useful when thinking about leadership.

You need to develop a thick skin. You need to be able to distinguish between what is justified criticism that you can adapt and use and what is unjustified – where you simply need to acknowledge the criticism and move on. This is not easy and is not really something that you can be taught, but it does come with experience. Nonetheless, when hearing the criticism, ask yourself, 'Would I say/feel the same in that position? Have I ever made similar comments about previous leaders I have worked for or alongside?' Are you over-reacting to someone's tone and manner and is your tone and manner upping the ante?

You need critical mass

The larger your organisation, the harder it is to win everyone over to the direction in which you want to take the organisation. Inevitably there will be those who don't agree. Sometimes that disagreement will be healthy and valid. Sometimes it will simply consist of those people who are generally resistant to change. And occasionally it will be those people who, for whatever reason, simply want to oppose anything that you try to do because they don't think that you are right for the organisation.

It is too easy in those circumstances to spend a great deal of time and energy on the minority who object or complain, and to neglect those people who are energised and optimistic about the future, or who are simply getting on with the job.

As a leader you rarely need unanimity. What you need is critical mass. If the majority of people are with you and what you are trying to achieve then that is usually enough. This means that despite the critics and naysayers (to paraphrase Richard Olivier) the organisation will move forward and this is where you need to be spending your energy. That is not to say that you don't give the others a fair hearing – they may actually have some important and useful points to make – but don't spend a disproportionate amount of energy on those you will never win over anyway.

No one will thank you

Actually this isn't entirely true. But you do need to develop an ability to assess your own performance as a leader and not to rely on others to remind you of what you are good at. Guess what – they won't. You need to know not just what you could do better, but, and probably more importantly, what you do well. An old chief exec of mine, John Garnett, used to say about moving into top leadership positions, 'You can't expect the salary *and* a round of applause!' Fair point. But, can I strongly suggest you find someone who will give you lots and lots of positive reinforcement? I talk more about this in Chapter 9 when I look at how to keep yourself sane.

Patience is a virtue

You will find that things take longer than you either want them to, or think they should. It is one of the endless frustrations of chief execs and, incidentally, trustees too. But things do have a way of happening in their own time. You can attempt to accelerate some things of course; however, unless the ingredients are right, the change process will almost always take longer than you have anticipated.

You will also find that you have to repeat the same messages over and over again, and still people will claim that you didn't tell them! Again, this is a natural function of workplaces, because there are people in them, and they will hear your messages when they are ready to or when you have created an environment that makes them want to listen. And even then, there will always be those who appear not to have got the message. I remember being told about the former Chief Executive of SAS Airways who used to talk about 'the thousand tellings'. You have to repeat, repeat, repeat. A simple analogy is when you fall in love and you and your partner tell each other that very first time that you love one another. All well and good – but having it said only once is rarely enough. Even though you know that your partner loves you, you need to hear it often and the same is true of messages in the workplace. Even if people do know something – the vision, progress against objectives, the values, how good they are – they still need to hear it regularly.

So you need to develop the kind of patience that keeps you going when things are not happening as fast as you would like, or when people appear not to have grasped the essentials of your messages.

Failure is inevitable

Many people will judge how successful you are as a leader on how successful the organisation is in that moment, and very often that will be about the money, even though the real test of an organisation in the voluntary sector is about the work that you do. That can be frustrating, I know, and it also makes it too easy to concentrate on the now forgetting what you have achieved and what you are planning to do for the future, because the concentration is on the immediate.

Paradoxically, you will of course be criticised if you don't think about the long term, even while being measured on the now. Despite all that pressure, you need to hang on to your vision and plans for tomorrow, next week, next year and the next decade.

All organisations go through cycles. None simply grow and grow without hitting crisis points. Sometimes it is true to say that the crises come about because of poor leadership, but more often there are external factors that can be hard to anticipate and hard to manage! You need neither to get over-excited or complacent about the good times nor to get overly despondent or worried about the tough times. Both tough times and good times come and go – and come and go, and come and go… 'This too will pass' is a good way of looking at the tough and the easy.

I am reminded of the Rudyard Kipling poem 'If' and, in particular, the lines:

> If you can meet with Triumph and Disaster
> And treat those two imposters just the same

You can't do it alone

I think, however, that probably the most important thing you need to remember is that you cannot do it alone. You simply must make sure that you have a management/leadership team around you that has established a common set of behaviours and values and that is working with you. It doesn't matter how well you are apparently leading from the top if this is not reflected in what is going on in the rest of the organisation. If the management team is not right, then your best efforts will come to naught. And if the team isn't right, then you simply have to move the members out of the organisation.

This is really, really hard to do and I have to admit that I have not done it well myself in the past. I have a tendency to think that I can win everyone over! But trust me, and not just me but your fellow chief execs and senior people – their stories are all similar. If you don't get the right people around you, you will find it extremely difficult to achieve what you are trying to do. And the right people are not the cleverest or most experienced in my view. The right people are the ones with the right attitudes. Skills can be taught, experience can be given. But a can-do mentality will serve you better in the long run and it's much harder to teach. I'm reminded of Channel 4's *SuperVet* where the owner and pet surgeon extraordinaire, Noel Fitzpatrick, says that his priority when recruiting vets and veterinary nurses is a big heart before a big brain. I think he's got a point.

What do you need to succeed?

I believe the single most important quality you need is courage. I penned the following 'Kiplingesque' short poem which I hope illustrates what I mean by this.

The quality which will serve you best
Is courage. So when you are pressed
Around by doubt and fear of what is new,
The courage of conviction will see you through.
Which, in the cold, hard waking hour,
Will hold your hope's inspiring power.
The courage to confess your wrong –
And thus redress, yet show you're strong.
The courage to allow the light
In others, so that they glow bright
Even if this casts you into shade
And no one knows the gift you gave.
The courage to look yourself in the eye
And know your weakness and your lie
And still go on believing in
Your courage to undo your sin.
The courage to speak up for what is right
Even if the ensuing fight
Costs your repute or livelihood,
Still, knowing what you do is good.
And not least of these the courage to know
If it's time to stay, or time to go.

Some critical dos and don'ts!

DO	DON'T
■ Praise	■ Pander
■ Get the right people on board	■ Hang on to people who are not helping you move forward
■ Trust your people and delegate well	■ Try to be the expert yourself
■ Surround yourself with trusted advisers	■ Pay too much attention to the negative minority
■ Appreciate people	■ Forget to recognise effort as well as achievement

2 Inspiring or perspiring?

By working faithfully eight hours a day, you may eventually get to be a boss and work twelve hours a day.
Attributed to both Robert Quillen and Robert Frost

Outcomes

After reading this chapter you will:
- Be clear about the distinction between management and leadership
- Have a good sense of your own leadership style
- Know how to adapt your style to help others to follow you

Are you doing the right things?

In a senior leadership role it is important to distinguish between management and leadership. They are not the same, although they are both equally important.

Someone once said that leadership is about getting extraordinary results out of ordinary people. Someone else said management is about doing things right – leadership is about doing the right thing.

I think these sayings sum up very nicely the difference between management and leadership. Management is essentially about resources, leadership is essentially about people.

The distinction between management and leadership

Managers	Leaders
Set objectives	Create vision
Human resources	People
Motivate	Inspire
Analyse	Imagine
Control	Release

The list above shows a polarised version of the difference between the two requirements of senior positions. The popular view at the moment is that leadership is more important than management. I don't share that view. My observation is that you need both. I have worked in my life for two people who had the extremes of management and leadership qualities. One was a superb manager: he followed all the rules and procedures, made sure we had plans, that our work was monitored and so on. The other was an absolutely inspirational leader: we were excited and enthused by his vision and ideas.

Interestingly, under both leaders we, the team, ended up demoralised and actually failing to achieve the task. In the first case, with the excellent manager, we lacked vision and excitement. When things got tough it wasn't enough to know that we were following all the right procedures. We wanted to know why – was it worth it? Sadly, he wasn't able to inspire us in the hard times.

In the second case, the vision wasn't enough. We had no clear plans, no specific objectives, no way of knowing if we were getting there. And, of course, we didn't achieve the vision.

So you need both. A vision is no good without a plan and a plan is no good without a vision.

Why should they follow you?

The American researchers and writers, Kouzes and Posner, talk about leadership as 'a reciprocal relationship between those who choose to lead and those who decide to follow'.

I think this is a useful description for a number of reasons. The first is that it stresses the idea of reciprocity. In other words, if people don't follow you then you clearly cannot be their leader.

Secondly, leadership is a conscious choice. To do the things that make you a good leader requires a commitment and courage greater than that of simply doing what is in the job description.

Thirdly, you can't force people to follow you. They have to choose to.

This is a particular challenge at the top, because you effectively have two tasks to do. You have to create an environment that allows your immediate team (i.e. your direct reports) to want to follow you. But you also have to be credible as a leader to those people further down the organisation, as well as your volunteers and supporters whom you may not have so much to do with on a daily basis.

Critically, you need to begin with those who report directly to you. If you are providing the right sort of leadership for them, and they are inspired and committed to what you are trying to achieve with the organisation, then they are more likely to disseminate the right sort of positive messages throughout their own teams or to their peers.

So what makes people want to choose to follow you? When I run my leadership training courses, I ask people to visualise the best leader they have ever worked for, someone who helped to make coming to work a pleasure, who made being committed and enthusiastic easy. Typically the lists look something like this:

Best Leader

- Listener
- Enthusiastic
- Open
- Sense of humour
- Commitment
- Trust in self and staff
- Knowledgeable
- Fair

- Focused
- Honest
- Didn't get angry about mistakes
- Let people get on with the job
- Loyal to the team

- *Good communicator*
- *Didn't take credit for others' ideas*
- *Praised frequently*
- *Willing to admit mistakes*
- *Took on other ideas*

Do you recognise any of these attributes when you think about the best leader you have ever worked with?

Then I ask people to visualise the very worst leader they have ever worked for. Usually this is much easier for them – they often joke that they are stuck for choice!

Worst leader

- Unfair
- Lazy
- Inconsistent
- Doesn't tell the truth
- Takes credit for others' work
- Doesn't listen

- Doesn't care about the staff
- Disloyal – isn't open
- Operates a blame culture
- Doesn't lead by example

- Status driven
- Incompetent
- Has favourites
- Doesn't take decisions
- Knows it all
- Doesn't trust the staff

Again, you probably recognise some of the words on this list too.

Now there are a number of points to make about these descriptions. The first is that, if you notice, most of the words are relationship based. In other words, they describe the emotional impact of that leader on the individuals describing them. Secondly, very few of the points in either category are about taking decisions, setting strategic objectives, monitoring results and so on. They are nearly all about relationships and how we felt around this person.

As followers, we judge our leaders almost entirely on their impact on us as individuals – rightly or wrongly.

Interestingly, when I ask the question, 'Did everyone in your organisation agree that this was the best/worst leader?', the answer is usually 'No'. If you think about your own examples, there's a pretty good chance that for those leaders who you thought of as good, there were others in your organisation or team who didn't share your view. The same is probably true for those who you thought were terrible.

So what makes the difference? Why do some people see the same leader as either good or bad? The answer is that it's all about perception.

I was doing some coaching work with a chief exec of a medium-sized voluntary organisation working with children with learning disabilities. This individual (whom I shall call Mark for the present), inherited two senior members of staff. One of these (let's call her Paula) thought that Mark was a great chief executive. The other (let's call him James) thought that Mark was terrible. Why? Mark, after all, was one individual, not Jekyll and Hyde.

As we worked it through we realised that the difference was one of perception. Mark's leadership style was forceful and direct. He didn't spend a lot of time agonising about the detail – he listened but made decisions very quickly. Paula had a very similar style and recognised that in him. James, on the other hand, was much more thoughtful and detailed in his approach. He found Mark hard to work with because he often felt that his views were not being considered seriously enough. When Paula had a one-to-one with Mark it lasted no more than about half an hour and was very action-focused. James needed more time. He wanted to talk through the documents/reports he had prepared in some detail.

Once Mark had recognised the dissonance between the needs of his two directors he was able to adapt his style to make James feel more appreciated. This in turn helped James find a way to follow him.

This issue of leadership style is an important one. You will often find that those people who think you are great appreciate your style and those who don't, don't!

So it's important that you are aware of how you operate, how others operate and how your own style may impact on others' desire to follow you. Those people who you find 'difficult' may only be difficult because they find it hard to follow you due to dissonance between your preferred style and theirs, not because there is any real, deep distance between what you and they aspire to achieve for the organisation.

Below is a leadership style test that I designed in order to help leaders think about how they lead others. I'm not a big fan of psychometric tests because I suspect they are used too much to label people and don't allow for people's ability to grow and learn. So I invented this one myself. It is simply a tool to get you to think. Unlike most tests of this type, you can cheat – if you don't like the answer it gives you then change your scores!

The point is that there is no right or wrong answer. The purpose of the test is to get you to think about the relationships you have with those you lead (and indeed those you seek to influence) and to discuss what you can do with your own style to adapt it to the needs of others.

Leadership style test

It is important that you fill in the questionnaire before looking ahead at the scoring instructions otherwise you will find that the scoring system influences how you score yourself.

Instructions

Look at one row at a time. Thinking about yourself in a leadership context, give each word a value from **1–4** with **4** representing the word most like you and **1** representing the word least like you. You must have one of each number only in every row so that each row adds up to 10. In other words, every line must contain a 4, a 3, a 2 and a 1.

Example

	Score		Score		Score		Score
Funny	4	Interesting	2	Quiet	1	Determined	3

The test

	Score		Score		Score		Score
Trusting		Precise		Enthusiastic		Quick	
Confident		Supportive		Careful		Creative	
Imaginative		Forceful		Responsive		Economical	
Methodical		Demonstrative		Competitive		Helpful	
Determined		Persuasive		Analytical		Receptive	
Adaptable		Practical		Encouraging		Courageous	
Objective		Empathetic		Inspiring		Animated	
Generous		Strong-willed		Mischievous		Factual	
Focused		Relaxed		Challenging		Experimental	
Fun		Action-oriented		Relationship focused		Questioning	

Copy your score from the original sheet onto this one, putting the score against the word. When you have done that, add up the scores for each shade and mark them against the boxes below. I use colours because I think they are the most evocative indicators – you'll have to imagine them here.

	Score		Score		Score		Score
Trusting		Precise		Enthusiastic		Quick	
Confident		Supportive		Careful		Creative	
Imaginative		Forceful		Responsive		Economical	
Methodical		Demonstrative		Competitive		Helpful	
Determined		Persuasive		Analytical		Receptive	
Adaptable		Practical		Encouraging		Courageous	
Objective		Empathetic		Inspiring		Animated	
Generous		Strong-willed		Mischievous		Factual	
Focused		Relaxed		Challenging		Experimental	
Fun		Action-oriented		Relationship focused		Questioning	

	Score			Score
GREEN			BLUE	
YELLOW			RED	

You will find that you have a slightly different score in each box. What does this mean? Well, if you look at the words in the 'green' boxes you can probably see that they are linked by people or feelings. The words in the 'blue' boxes are linked by facts or information. The words in the 'yellow' boxes are linked by ideas or creativity and the words in the 'red' boxes are linked by action or results. The higher your score in a particular area the more likely it is that your style is dominated by those words.

For example, if your dominant score is 'red', then you probably come across as quite fast, not interested in detail, want to just get on with it – which is fine, except for those people who want to consider the detail, take more time to come to a decision and so on.

The point is that none of the styles is right or wrong. It's just that someone may not respond well to your leadership, not because either you or they are awful (although you might be!), but because your style and theirs differ.

You can sit on your high horse saying, 'Well, I'm the Boss so we do it my way'. But actually, that doesn't work. If you want people to follow you, you need to adapt your way of being with them to what they need – not what you want to give.

Don't think so much in terms of 'do as you would be done by' because that assumes that everyone wants the same as you. A more effective way of thinking is probably to 'do to others as they would have done to themselves' (or something like that!).

So how people perceive your leadership will be highly dependent upon how they see your style. Some will see it positively and some will see it negatively. None of these perceptions is necessarily true about you, but they do reflect how you are seen, and so they are true for the person experiencing your leadership.

The following is simply a summary of how you might be perceived by people who have styles that are different from yours.

	When viewed positively could be seen as	*When viewed negatively could be seen as*
GREEN **Feelings/ relationships**	■ Caring ■ Supportive ■ Interested in individuals ■ Nurturing ■ Cares about relationships ■ Warm ■ Good listener	■ Overly nurturing ■ Misplaced loyalties ■ Puts individuals over the task ■ Not letting people grow or make their own mistakes ■ Hangs on to poor performers ■ Too soft
BLUE **Facts/ information**	■ Practical ■ Pays attention to details ■ Gets the facts right ■ Makes clear logical decisions ■ Authoritative ■ Takes time to think	■ Too much order ■ Overly attentive to detail ■ Never gets anything done ■ Always plays by the rules ■ Closed-minded ■ Overly focused on facts
YELLOW **Ideas/ change**	■ Enthusiastic ■ Creative – prepared to experiment ■ Fun to work with ■ Open-minded ■ Ready to challenge the status quo ■ Looks for new possibilities	■ Addicted to change ■ Starts things and doesn't finish them ■ Lots of initiatives all at once ■ Doesn't get results ■ Doesn't see things through
RED **Action/ results**	■ Confident ■ Quick ■ Gets results ■ Dynamic ■ Focused ■ Inspiring	■ Action only ■ Not concerned about individuals ■ Doesn't listen well ■ Bullying ■ Doesn't think things through

The above positive and negative characteristics are of course generalisations. All people are different and will have a mix of characteristics. However, determining how you like to lead and recognising that others may have different perceptions about your style may help you to be a more effective leader.

You may use lots of different styles and approaches when you are leading people, but it's still you, your character and your personality. You are simply adopting the appropriate behaviours for the particular moment.

How to use the styles

With your team

This questionnaire works with leadership teams at all levels so why not get your team to fill in the questionnaire at your next meeting? Have a discussion about what the differences mean and how you can all be more tolerant and understanding of one another. A word of warning, however. Don't ask people to fill it in about each other. People can get very hurt if they think they are being misunderstood, and it may be that the perception they have of themselves is widely different from that which others have of them. Much better to get people to self-evaluate.

For groups

A number of years ago we were introducing a new database system into our organisation. This was a fairly radical change and would require our people to work quite differently from how they had in the past, in order to make the most of the new system. When we briefed the project, we had to be sure that we engaged people's commitment by speaking to their particular needs.

So we began by explaining that this was a brand new system which would require new ways of working and thinking (the yellow category), and that it was capable of capturing a great deal of data (the blue category)

about our customers which would potentially make our service to them better and make it easier for staff to operate (the green category). And of course all of this would mean we would get better results (the red category). All of this we genuinely believed.

The point is that when you are doing your big leadership briefings and you are seeking buy-in, make sure that you are using all four languages. That way you are much more likely to create an atmosphere where the majority of people will feel more able to follow your plan.

For individuals

You don't have to get people to fill in the leadership style questionnaire in order to adapt your style to theirs. Sometimes it is obvious what style people prefer from the way in which they approach you. But the simplest thing is to recognise when your communication with them is not working well and to experiment with your approach until you find the one that works.

Action-centred leadership

The principle of action-centred leadership was developed by John Adair at Sandhurst during the 1960s. Although leadership models have moved on since then, there are many useful aspects of the action-centred leadership model which stand the test of time and will help you to lead your organisation more effectively. Its beauty lies in its simplicity. It describes quite clearly what you need to do, and when, and it should undoubtedly be a key part of your leadership tool box. When I am really stuck I go to this checklist, and it has yet to let me down.

Action-centred leadership says that there are three interdependent areas on which leaders need to focus.

The successful leader recognises that these three activities need to be achieved in balance with one another. Overly focusing on the task at the expense of building the team or developing individuals will result in demotivated individuals and a disconnected team, which of course will ultimately affect the task.

Leaders who put the individuals before the task are not leading from a position of strength. You are not the representative of your people – you are their leader and that means that occasionally the task will have to come first and the needs of the team must be put to the back.

You, as the leader at the top of the organisation, need to ensure that all these three things are in place. So you need to make sure, as far as you are able, that you have the necessary systems, processes and resources for the task to be achieved, the individuals to feel developed and recognised and the teams to work together effectively.

The following framework summarises the key activities.

Key Actions		Task	Team	Individual
Define objectives		Identify tasks and constraints	Hold team meetings; share commitment	Clarify objectives; gain acceptance
Plan	Gather information	Consider options Check resources	Consult Develop suggestions Encourage ideas Assess skills	
	Decide	Priorities Timescales Standards	Structure	Allocate tasks Delegate Set targets
Brief		Clarify objectives Describe plan	Explain decisions Answer questions Check understanding	Listen Enthuse
Monitor/support		Assess progress Maintain standards	Co-ordinate Reconcile conflict	Advise Assist/reassure Counsel Discipline
Evaluate		Summarise Review objectives Replan if necessary	Recognise and gain from success Learn from mistakes	Appraise performance
			Guide, train and give praise	

Reproduced from *The Manager as a Leader*, Industrial Society Press, 1989

I find the framework is most useful when it appears something isn't going quite according to plan. A quick look over it will very often show something that may have been missed. For example, if a particular objective isn't being achieved, is it because it wasn't briefed clearly? Were the jobs appropriately allocated? Did you delegate effectively? And so on.

You can translate this relatively simple model for use at the top of the organisation.

Achieving the task
- Clarify the vision and remind people of it constantly.
- Check progress against mission and objectives.
- Ensure that the organisation's departments/teams have clear objectives that are measurable and relevant to the bigger picture (i.e. the vision and mission), and ensure that you monitor regularly by asking your line managers to report on progress.

Building the team(s)

I will talk specifically about building a senior management team in Chapter 5. Here I concentrate on your actions as a leader at the top of the organisation to support team building throughout your organisation.

- Encourage managers to have regular meetings with their teams.
- Praise team performances.
- Assess the senior team's progress against team objectives.
- Involve teams in developing the overall strategy.
- Encourage managers and staff to build in some time to have fun.

Developing the individuals

- 'Walk the job' (see Chapter 4).
- Ensure that the organisation has an effective and easy-to-use appraisal system and that managers are implementing it.
- Set aside money for training.
- Introduce an acting in absence system so that when a manager is away a member of their team acts for them, attends meetings on their behalf and so on.
- Speak to as many of your staff as individuals as you can (I have a relatively small organisation so I have a one-to-one with every single member of staff once a year so that they have the opportunity to talk to me directly).
- Be prepared, on occasion, to roll up your sleeves and get stuck in. But don't make it a habit. You should not become a resource that they rely on. You need to be doing your job – not theirs!

Leading by example

As a leader you need to set for your people the example you want them to follow. That means you need to practise what you preach. But first you need to be clear about what sort of example it is that you want to set.

The following questionnaire should help you to think about what might be involved. These are just some generic examples of what could be required in setting a good example. Undoubtedly, there will be ones that are specific to your organisation. Where you score low, you need to take action.

Setting a good example
Self-assessment: how well do the following statements describe you?

1   I have communicated to everyone what I think good practice is

Low   Medium   High

1	2	3	4	5	6	7	8	9	10

2   I always adhere to what I think is good practice

Low   Medium   High

1	2	3	4	5	6	7	8	9	10

3   I never cancel appointments or meetings with my staff

Low   Medium   High

1	2	3	4	5	6	7	8	9	10

4   My team has clearly set goals which I monitor monthly

Low   Medium   High

1	2	3	4	5	6	7	8	9	10

5   I take accountability for my own and others' mistakes

Low   Medium   High

1	2	3	4	5	6	7	8	9	10

6   I am always calm and positive

Low   Medium   High

1	2	3	4	5	6	7	8	9	10

7   I can control my body language so that my staff don't know when I am feeling stressed/negative or tired

Low   Medium   High

1	2	3	4	5	6	7	8	9	10

8   I have a good work/life balance

Low   Medium   High

1	2	3	4	5	6	7	8	9	10

9   I am very clear about my personal philosophy of leadership

Low   Medium   High

1	2	3	4	5	6	7	8	9	10

10   My staff are very clear about what my leadership philosophy is

Low   Medium   High

1	2	3	4	5	6	7	8	9	10

Modelling

At the end of the day, what you are doing by setting a good example is modelling the behaviour you want others to engage in. I would start by thinking of those people who you consider to be good leaders and copy what they did that impressed you. Then consistently model the behaviour you would like others to exhibit. Some examples might include:

- Turn up to meetings on time.
- Don't work late – leave work at the normal time.
- 'Walk the job'.
- Talk positively about situations, including negative ones.
- Listen to people – woes and all – and take account of personal details such as children, holidays and hobbies.
- Demonstrate enthusiasm with your tone, your questions and your body language.

There will be others that are relevant to your work situation.

Behaviour

I can remember sitting in on a senior team meeting where the chief executive was talking about a change to the structure of the outreach team and he asked for feedback on his proposed changes. No one said anything, but the director of outreach programmes looked distinctly upset. It was obvious that he wasn't happy. However, the chief exec ignored it on the basis that the director could have spoken up if he had wanted to. And of course he should have done. And he probably wished he had. But, as my grandmother used to say, 'if wishes were horses, beggars would ride'.

You won't be surprised to hear that the proposed changes didn't work well; it was obvious from the body language of the director of outreach programmes that he didn't want them implemented.

The moral of the story is that it helps if you ask people what they're thinking and at the same time observe their body language. If someone is looking negative, ask them about it. You don't have to be confrontational; simply saying something like 'You look a little unsure about this, John' or 'You seem unenthusiastic about this, Mary' will often prompt people to speak up. People can obfuscate with words, but rarely with body language. And normally, when it's obvious, they really do genuinely want you to ask them what they think. And if you do ask them, they are much more likely to tell you what they have been thinking. If they then say that they're happy with it – well, they are more likely to make it work, and at the very least you will be able to point out to them that when you asked, they raised no problems.

Distributed leadership

At the top of the organisation what you absolutely must do is grow the leadership skills and abilities of your people. And not just the members of your senior team – but all those who show any aptitude in this area. Succession planning isn't about nobbling some poor soul to take over from you once you finally keel over or get booted out! It's about making sure that the skills and attributes needed are shared and grown in your organisation. That means giving people both training and opportunities, particularly opportunities to lead on projects or stand in for their managers. Have a written policy so people understand its purpose and the limits of authority. This is DSC's policy:

Acting in absence policy
Who is covered by this policy?
Line managers.

What is covered by this policy?
This policy outlines the procedure to be followed to ensure planned staff absence is covered effectively.

The policy
To ensure continuity of leadership and accountability for delivery in any given team, DSC has a policy of appointing an individual to act in absence for any line manager or other member of the team who is absent on leave or anticipated sickness.
Acting in absence has the added benefit for the line manager of developing leadership and management skills within their team, and enables the individual to learn new skills and build their confidence and experience.

Acting in absence procedure
1. The line manager identifies a member of staff who they wish to act in absence.
2. A discussion is held to clarify the staff member's willingness to take on the acting in absence role. If the staff member is unwilling the line manager will choose someone else. This may sometimes be a staff member or line manager from another team.
3. A meeting is scheduled immediately prior to the cover period for the manager to fully brief the staff member concerned on what activities, actions and priorities are planned during their absence and to clarify levels of authority.
4. If appropriate, the staff member may be required to attend the monthly leadership team meeting and carry out subsequent staff briefing (even if the line manager has returned).
5. The line manager will brief the rest of the team about who is acting in absence and will reinforce that the nominated staff member has the same level of authority, for the period of acting in absence, as the manager.
6. The line manager will let the organisation know (via an email) who is acting in absence while they are away.
7. The line manager will ensure that their out of office message and voicemail states who is acting in absence for them.
8. Upon return from leave the line manager and the staff member will have a handover/de-brief meeting within two days.

9. In the event, for whatever reason, the nominated staff member is unable to take a decision or carry out a piece of work, they will seek help and guidance from their senior manager.
10. In the event that the staff member is taken ill unexpectedly, the senior manager will decide who will act in absence.

Part of your planning for the future has to be about making sure that others know how to lead. And if they know how to lead, I promise, it will make your job as a leader much, much easier.

And don't forget to keep *thinking* about leadership. Read books and articles, go on courses, network with others doing the same sort of role. Listen, learn and adapt.

Some critical dos and don'ts!

DO	DON'T
■ Concentrate on how you can adapt your style to others	■ Get stuck in only one way of leading
■ Get your team to think about their own style of leading/interacting	■ Assume others can't change their styles if need be
■ Remember there are three areas you need to deliver on	■ Overly concentrate on one particular aspect of a team, task or individual
■ Think about what kind of example you want to set	■ Forget to encourage the rest of your senior team to do the same
■ Question people in response to their body language	■ Ignore obvious non-verbal signs of upset or resistance

3 No vision, no insight

If you want to build a ship, then don't drum up men to gather wood, give orders and divide the work. Rather, teach them to yearn for the far and endless sea.

Attributed to Antoine de Saint-Exupéry

Outcomes

After reading this chapter you will:
- **Know the distinction between vision, mission and strategic objectives**
- **Know how to establish what they are**
- **Know how to involve people in creating them**

One of the key things that you need to do at the top of the organisation is to ensure that there is a vision and that people know what it is. To be honest, I don't think it matters that much whether that vision has been developed by you, your trustees or has always existed. Your job is to make sure that there is one, that it is communicated and understood by your staff and volunteers and, above all, that you personally believe in it and are committed to it.

There is a lot of confusion about the difference between vision, mission, aims and objectives. Forgetting about the semantics for the moment, essentially there are three things organisations need in order to be successful:

1. A clear idea of what their world will look like if the organisation achieves its dream (a vision of the future).
2. A specific long-term target to work towards (the mission).
3. A number of identified activities that people can work on which will help to achieve the mission and ultimately the vision (the objectives).

Vision

The most pathetic person in the world is someone who has sight but no vision.

Attributed to Helen Keller

Do organisations really need visions to survive? And what are they really for? Well, actually, lots of organisations have lost sight of their vision (if you'll pardon the pun!) and yet continue to operate perfectly well. But organisations that have lost their vision do have a certain number of symptoms – do you recognise any of these?

- General resistance to change.
- General low morale.
- Tendency to want to give up when things go wrong.
- Focus on internal mechanisms.
- Sense that the organisation exists to serve the staff not the beneficiaries.
- Higher than normal levels of gossip and backbiting.
- A lot of bureaucracy.

The typical pattern in the voluntary sector is that an individual spots an injustice, wants to help someone or engage in supporting some cause and has a vision about what they want to do about it. So the origins of most voluntary sector organisations lie in the very clear vision of an individual. As the individual succeeds in doing something about their cause, typically they begin attracting funding for it and then they begin to employ people. As time goes on, movement takes place from, for example, one individual wanting to do something to help blind people, to a large organisation, such as the RNIB – a big national charity that employs thousands of people, is helped by lots of volunteers and attracts large sums of money. And it's often along that route that the vision gets lost and the organisation's focus centres on what it is doing rather than why it is doing it.

Visions unite people. I've always thought (but my editor tells me otherwise) that Voltaire said, 'to unite men and women you need to give them cathedrals to build'. In other words, human beings need a sense of a higher purpose, something that helps them to believe that what they are doing is worthwhile. And if they share that vision, that higher purpose, it unites them and inspires them to put in their best efforts. I think the following apocryphal story describes this beautifully.

> A man is walking along a building site and he comes across three workers who are laying bricks on top of bricks. The first worker is working quite slowly, without a great deal of enthusiasm and has only managed to lay a few bricks. The man asks the worker, 'What are you doing?' and the worker replies, somewhat jadedly, 'Can't you see? I'm laying bricks on top of bricks'.
>
> The man continues along until he comes to the second worker who is working much faster than the first and has laid several rows of bricks. He asks her the same question to which the response this time is, 'I'm building a wall'. The man then comes across the third worker who is working at three times the pace of the other two, has built an entire wall, a corner and a window space and is whistling cheerily at the same time. This time the answer to the question is, 'I'm helping to build a cathedral'.

I have come across many definitions of 'vision'. Ben Thompson-McCausland, a vision consultant, has spoken on the subject in many speeches. He talks about vision as an ambitious dream, which is communicable, achievable, memorable and inspirational. Richard Field, former Chairman of J&J Dyson, was a speaker at the leadership programme I used to run and described a vision as something that is stretching, credible, inspiring and memorable.

What all people engaged in working on vision agree is that it is a realisable dream – a desired future state, something to which an organisation aspires. It is the 'why' of the activity that your organisation exists for. It acts as the touchstone.

It is the thing that helps you to identify what your priorities are when making decisions because the decisions you make should be those that are helping you towards realising your dream. Above all it needs to inspire, be memorable and be something that everyone in the organisation can identify with.

One of the key things that all gurus say about vision is that it isn't measurable. It is not an objective or intention and should never be designed or amended by accountants! And it should be expressed in the language of the everyday. People aren't generally inspired by statements such as 'our vision is to ensure a socially coherent, economically vibrant community which minimises social exclusion and maximises effective regeneration of blah de blah de blah...'

For starters, what on earth does that mean? Actually it means a happy, well-off bunch of people who get on well and care about their community, doesn't it? Simple language that touches the heart is the most effective language of vision. Martin Luther King said, 'I have a dream...' He didn't say, 'I have a re-engineered strategic plan for changing a paradigm'.

For Jews, Christians and Muslims, one of the memorable visions was the vision of Israel – a land of milk and honey – given by Moses to the 12 tribes. I've never heard it said that the elders came back to Moses and said, 'OK, but only if the milk is semi-skimmed and the honey comes from organic bees!'

A vision is not a business plan. It is a simple statement of what the world will look like once you have finished your work.

A vision is the desired unmeasurable, unquantifiable, future state that you wish your organisation to achieve. Having identified the vision, all the other management speak is simply a way of defining how you go about working towards achieving your vision. So you identify a mission (also an aim) which you then break down into specific objectives which are then further broken down into plans.

To return to our Moses example, his vision coming out of Egypt was 'a land of milk and honey'. The mission was to reach the Promised Land and the objectives were things such as getting across the Red Sea.

The vision shouldn't be a strapline. In fact, really the vision is not for people outside your organisation. It is for your staff and volunteers, in order to inspire them in their daily activities. So you are not necessarily trying to come up with some statement that will please a funder, or a supporter. For these groups of people you express the vision and activity of your organisation in whatever language is going to get you the money or the support. The real vision statement is for you and your people: your staff, your volunteers, your trustees.

I have observed that the most successful organisations are those that have visions that broadly fit the following criteria:

- They are inspiring.
- They are believable: they fit the context of the organisation.
- They feel achievable – even if not in this lifetime.
- They are rarely longer than seven to ten words.
- They are memorable.
- They use simple, everyday language which people can understand and identify with.
- They describe a picture of the future and avoid infinitives such as 'to help'.
- They stand the test of time: they are usually big enough to cope with the changing environment in which the organisation is operating.

So, a vision sets the overall context by which individuals can connect with the organisation and helps them to create new possibilities for it. Above all, having a simple vision statement helps you to 'speak possibility into being'. In other words, things become possible that wouldn't have been before because people now have something to work towards.

Below are some examples of visions that I have collected on my travels around the UK voluntary sector. They were developed by the people who worked in the organisations concerned as part of a training programme – so they may not be the official vision of the charity concerned – but they are the visions that inspired the people who came up with them.

Early Years Scotland
Confident happy children

International Voluntary Service
A world at peace

National Museums of Scotland
Inspired, educated people with a sense of the past

Kibble Education and Care Centre
A future for young people with a past

Scotland's First National Park
Local folk working together in their community

Together Trust
A safe place and new future for vulnerable children

Knowsley Community Empowerment Network
Government decisions shaped by the community

Lincoln Welcome Asylum Seeker Support Group
Safely at home in a welcoming city

SoundLINKS
Sound opportunities for all

Creative and Supportive Trust
Women ex-offenders leading positive lives

Artangel
People appreciating contemporary art

Cruse Bereavement Care
Life after death

Ely Museum
People with a sense of history

Action for Young Carers
Young carers with a life of their own

Nottingham Central Women's Aid
Strong, confident women

And my two particular favourites!!

Young Single Homeless Project
Yooves wiv rooves (sic)

Age Cymru Swansea
Sex and sangria for senior citizens in Swansea

How to create a vision

As you can see from above, the simpler the language and the shorter the sentence the more powerful and inspiring the statement can be for people. So what prevents us from having short, inspiring statements? Usually, trying to create a vision with the involvement of a committee. It is generally best to avoid having too many people involved with coming up with the final wording. This is because people are terribly attached to their particular words and find it difficult to let go. And that's when you end up with a vision statement which is several paragraphs of big, long words that people don't actually understand – but no one wants to say so.

Having said that, however, you do need to *involve* people in the development of the vision. There are a number of reasons for this. Firstly, they will have thoughts and ideas that you don't have, that are likely to make the vision more powerful. Secondly, if they have had no involvement it is much harder for them to buy into it.

Nonetheless, the final putting together of the words probably needs to be done by you. And at the very least the vision has to be something to which you personally are deeply committed. It shows if you're not.

My advice with developing a vision is to keep the process very simple. The following process works whatever the size of your organisation; you just need to adapt it accordingly.

Stage 1: Buy into the concept of vision

Begin with your trustees. Have a conversation with your chair about the vision of the organisation and how important it is that it is still relevant and meaningful. Put an item on the agenda of the next board meeting asking questions along the lines of 'What is our vision currently? Do we all agree with it? Do we all understand the same thing when we hear it? Is it still relevant today?' Ensure that you share with them what the whole concept of vision is about in the first place. Many people confuse vision with mission statements and business plans. Clear that up first.

Stage 2: Consult, round 1

If you are a small organisation, gather all your people together in one room. If you are larger, get your managers to meet with their teams. Tell them that you are looking at the vision of the organisation, want their help and input, and ask questions such as:

- What is special about this organisation?
- What do we want to achieve?
- Who are we trying to serve?
- How do we want the world/beneficiaries' lives to be different as a result of the work that we do?

Capture the critical words and use them to inform your thinking. Tell people that you will be working on it and will come back to them with further thoughts.

Stage 3: Come up with a statement

You and maybe one or two others thrash out the statement. At one organisation I worked with, the chief exec and the chair of trustees went away and came up with a statement, on which they consulted the rest of the trustees. They asked their fellow trustees to focus on the 'spirit' of the statement, i.e. what it was conveying, and not to get too distracted by the actual words. This worked well.

Also, don't let the size of the vision scare people into not having one. So many great ideas get scuppered because some bright spark says, 'But, if we grow our membership base by 100,000 we won't have the resources to deal with it!' Well firstly, wouldn't it be great if we were faced with that problem, rather than the one of not having enough members! And secondly, if it does grow, you'll also grow the resources to meet the demand. Honestly. You will.

The elders didn't say to Moses (well, as far as I know – I wasn't there), 'What if we haven't got enough cups for people to drink the milk out of? We don't have anything to clean sticky fingers with when they've eaten all the honey!'

Stage 4: Consult, round 2

Share what you have come up with with your staff and volunteers and ask for their opinions or ways in which it might be amended. Again, focus on the spirit of the statement, not the actual words.

Stage 5: Communicate infinity times!

Once you have decided what your vision is you need to communicate it over and over again. It needs to be on posters, at the top of internal documents, referred to at staff meetings, team meetings, senior management meetings and trustee meetings. Discuss your ongoing achievements using the vision as the backdrop. Remind people. Remind people. Remind people.

Mission

You will probably either remember, or have heard of, the famous words spoken by John F. Kennedy, President of the United States, in a speech in 1961: 'I believe that this nation should commit itself to achieving the goal, before this decade is out, of landing a man on the moon and returning him safely to the earth'. This is often paraphrased as 'A man on the moon by the end of the decade' and noted as an example of an inspiring vision but, actually, this isn't a vision at all. It is more like a mission or aim. The vision was one that the Americans shared with the Russians, perhaps even the whole of the world, which was unspoken but nonetheless mutually understood, something along the lines of 'Humankind in space'.

The mission is effectively the single big goal that will help you to achieve your vision. It's like a milestone on the way. So 'a man on the moon by the end of the decade' is one of the things that could be done to help achieve the overall vision of 'Humankind in space'. For the Russians, you could say that the mission was 'a man orbiting the earth' (i.e. Yuri Gagarin).

Missions are always measurable, but again expressed in simple, easy-to-understand language.

For example:
Vision: All children in Barkham have access to a good education.
Mission: To provide all children with learning disabilities in the Barkham area with access to specialised educational help by the end of 2020.

Again, the trick with deciding on what the core mission is is to keep it simple. What's the one big thing that the organisation could achieve which would be a big step towards achieving the vision?

Unlike vision, mission statements are usually measurable and quantifiable. They will frequently have a timescale attached to them.

Objectives

This is much more straightforward, as most of us are used to setting specific objectives. Be sure that the objectives are closely linked to the actions that you need to take in order to achieve the mission. If an objective isn't going to help achieve the mission then you need to test its validity in the context of your own organisation.

For example:
Vision: All children in Barkham have access to a good education.
Mission: To provide all children with learning disabilities in the Barkham area with access to specialised educational help by the end of 2020.
Objectives:
1. By the end of the year to have developed a relationship with the local authority so that they are factoring our proposals into their plans.
2. To create a parents' group for the Barkham area which is attended by at least 60% of those parents whose children could be part of the programme.
3. To develop a range of training materials which help teachers to facilitate the learning of children with special needs.

And so on...

The trick with all this is simplicity. The temptation is to make your plans, including the vision, mission and objectives, look sophisticated and complex, not least because often trustees like that. But at the end of the day your people need to understand what the organisation is trying to do, how it plans to do it and where they fit in.

And you need to revisit your vision, and its associated mission and strategic objectives, regularly. At DSC our vision of 'an independent voluntary sector at the heart of social change' hasn't changed much over the decades. But we check that it is still valid every couple of years when we are thinking about our long-term future. And we adapt our mission or strategic objectives to suit the environment that we are in at any one particular time.

Summary of key points

Vision	Humankind in space
Mission	A man on the moon by the end of the decade
Objectives	Build a rocket
	Train astronauts
	Invent rocket fuel, space suits, etc.

Some critical dos and don'ts!

DO

- Involve people in thinking about what the vision is
- Clarify for your trustees and staff the difference between vision, mission and objectives
- Keep the vision simple and inspiring
- Make sure that the mission and objectives are a way of achieving the vision
- Remind people, remind people, remind people

DON'T

- Write the vision by committee
- Get hung up on semantics – as long as you have these three things it doesn't matter that much what you call them
- Forget to keep revisiting it
- Forget to monitor how you are doing against the vision, not just the business plan!
- Believe that putting the vision on a poster or the front page of the strategic plan is how it is communicated

4 Gossip, grapevines and team talks

The great enemy of communication...is the illusion of it.
William Hollingsworth Whyte, American author

Outcomes

After reading this chapter you will:

- **Know how to manage the hidden communication channels**
- **Have some ideas about how to implement formal communication mechanisms**
- **Have a sense of how effective your own listening is**

Informal communication mechanisms

As someone at the top of the organisation, you are communicating all the time – whether you realise it or not. You are constantly being observed. Your behaviour, what you say and how you say it and your general demeanour are being scrutinised and noted, whether consciously or not. This chapter looks at the ways in which you communicate messages, formally and informally.

Organisations are not machines. They are unpredictable in how they behave. And the behaviour of organisations is influenced by the people within them. Self-evident you might say. But what influences the behaviour of the people? The information they gather and the communication processes they use. This is not straightforward. So much communication goes terribly wrong in organisations because we have not thought about what it is that we need to communicate, who needs to know and why they need to know it. Neither have we remembered that in the absence of information from the top, people will work it out, and often get it wrong.

I find it useful to think about organisational communication as if it's an ecosystem. Every part of it is connected to every other part in some way, and the whole and the parts are connected to the external world. And often the connections are not obvious or apparent. How is it that something you thought was confidential is being talked about in the corridor? Or something that you thought was fairly straightforward suddenly blows up and becomes a hot topic or source of contention?

Despite all our efforts to design intelligently our communication mechanisms by putting in structures and reporting lines, at the end of the day the structure is only as good as what the people working within it know and understand. That is not to say that it isn't worth spending time thinking about organisational structures, because of course a structure can either support your work or collapse under the weight of it. But the critical thing is to be constantly alive to the hidden structures in your organisation.

What are the hidden structures?

The hidden structures are the informal networks through which, minute by minute, information passes between people, teams and virtual communities. Within these networks people create and experience the culture, environment and work ethic of an organisation and share their celebrations and heartaches. Unfortunately, because they feel so nebulous it is too easy to ignore them and focus on what appears to be proper communication channels, such as emails and intranet.

Gossip

The first mechanism that supports this hidden structure is gossip, or the grapevine. And it is called the grapevine for a good reason: it grows extremely fast, gets into all sorts of nooks and crannies and is very strong! So what is gossip? Well, it's the informal chats that people have by the kettle, in the pub, in the corridor, or via email, other forms of electronic communication or social media.

People want to be able to talk about each other, particularly about what is happening to them. And they want to talk about their bosses. Part of this talking is to check out what other people think, see if it coincides with their own thinking and to jointly establish what the accepted view of a particular person or a particular situation is in the organisation. We all do this. So gossip is not an inherently bad thing.

Human beings are programmed to interact socially. With the exception of the few sociopaths in the world, all of us, even those of us who primarily communicate online, end up needing human contact. And we are programmed to interact through the medium of gossip. I mean gossip not necessarily in its negative sense (i.e. whispers and hurtful innuendo) but simply people talking about other people.

So we have established that gossip in and of itself is not necessarily deliberately malicious, but a way of building relationships through the exchange of information. Unfortunately, because many of us in leadership roles are oblivious to, or deliberately ignore, its existence, gossip can often get out of hand. And your best efforts to communicate the truth to people can be hijacked by an unfortunately timed or well-placed piece of gossip.

Gossip tends to get out of hand if there is a lack of information from the leadership team about what is going on. That's both formal/set communication and informal routes.

You need to know what people are talking about. What's on the grapevine? What is in people's heads? That's not to say you should have spies about the place, although it does help to have someone reliable who will let you know what the general mood is. But in a sense, you actually need to be part of it. I don't mean that you join in the gossip – but you need to be sufficiently well connected to hear what's going on. That means don't lock yourself in the office: hang out in the kitchen with the staff occasionally, go to the pub once in a while. Walk around the building saying 'hi' to people informally. Ask them what they think about a particular issue. Don't restrict all your communication with your people to formal occasions and *do not rely on email or other virtual communication mechanisms*!

Who is your 'political journalist'?

The journalist and TV presenter Andrew Marr wrote an excellent book, *My Trade*, which I highly recommend. Among many other useful and interesting revelations about the world of the media, he talks about the difficult balance that political journalists have to maintain in trying to get close to politicians in order to really know what's going on, while at the same time remaining sufficiently independent in order to be objective in their reporting.

He makes the point that if journalists get too close to politicians, they start to gain some insight into what some of the problems are that they face and this inevitably leads to sympathy and understanding, which has the potential to blunt the journalist's ability to go on the attack when necessary.

> a Chequers invitation…can make the recipient just that little bit more understanding of the problems facing the prime minister than he or she otherwise might be…If you really talk with a politician about their in tray, and the problems of rival departments, or of dodgy initiatives, it is hard to avoid seeing things their way. The same perspective that gives you insight also blunts your hostility.

I think this is a useful analogy in organisations generally. You too will have your political journalists: the ones who take what you say and interpret it for the 'masses'. And the less they understand of the real issues that are facing you in leading the organisation, the more likely it is that their interpretations of what you are doing will be negative. You need to make sure that you are explaining openly and honestly what is going on, what you are trying to achieve and why. Make a particular point of sharing information with your political journalist. This isn't about being manipulative, it's about common sense. If you don't tell people what's going on and what the problems are, how on earth do you expect them to be enthusiastic and supportive?

You can identify your political journalists fairly easily. They're often very popular with staff, the ones who are the centre of attention in the pub, the ones who people go to most often to question.

Behaviour

> The most important thing in communication is to hear what isn't being said.
> Attributed to Peter F. Drucker, management guru

The second key mechanism that supports the hidden structures is behaviour, that is, the observed body language, tone of voice and facial responses to information that people notice and which influences how they think about and react to what is going on around them.

The look on your face, the posture of your body, the speed with which you walk through the office, the tone of your voice, all of these things influence what people think. If you look cross and worried then they will assume that there is something to be cross and worried about – and that it's probably serious. If you look positive and enthusiastic, then guess what? They'll assume that there is much to be hopeful about. Do not underestimate the power that your behaviour, expressed largely through your body language, has on those around you.

Not only that, but people believe what they see rather than what they hear. If I were to say to you that this paper is pink with green spots would you believe what I say or what you see? If you want people to behave in a certain way then you need to behave in that same way. There is an apocryphal story about a woman who wanted her son to stop eating sugar. So she took the boy to see Gandhi and asked him to ask her son to stop eating sugar. Gandhi said he couldn't do it then, but asked her to bring her son back in a couple of weeks. When she returned, he told the boy to stop eating sugar. The woman was puzzled and asked him why he couldn't have said that two weeks ago. Gandhi replied that two weeks ago he, Gandhi, had been eating sugar.

Wherever this story came from, it's a great one. If you want your staff to be positive then you have to be positive. If you want them to go home on time then you have to go home on time. If you want them to listen to critical feedback then you have to listen to critical feedback. You will influence more by your general behaviour than you ever will through laying down rules or giving briefings.

Inevitably, however, there will be days when you are less able to display your anger, anxiety, frustration, etc. in an appropriately 'leaderly' way. So, sometimes, you simply need to know when *not* to be seen because in that moment it is too hard to manage your behaviour.

Don't forget that it's also about your more general appearance. There's no point bleating about how unfair and wrong it is for people to judge others by what they wear. The fact is that we do. Don't distract from your credibility by assuming that you, at the top, can get away with not looking the part. Don't give people a reason to make negative judgements about you based on how you're presenting yourself. If you want them to focus on what you have to say rather than what you look like then don't give them an opportunity to be distracted by something as daft as the fact you're wearing a T-shirt to work. And I'm not talking about suits here – just look as if you made an effort!

These messages are the ones that you should discuss and agree with your senior team and managers. Do you spend time with them talking about how they behave? Have you discussed how information is communicated simply through what their facial expression is when they walk out of a management meeting? Have you talked about looking the part? When you discuss the messages you are giving your staff and volunteers, do not ignore the hidden messages given out by behaviour and body language because people will believe those messages more than what you say.

During the Labour government of the nineties and new millennium we kept being told that the then Chancellor, Gordon Brown, and the then Prime Minister, Tony Blair, said that there was no problem in their relationship. But we knew that there was. How? Because it was screamingly obvious when you observed their body language when they were around each other or talking about each other.

Of all the various things that can help or hinder you in achieving your organisation's vision, these two – gossip and behaviour – are the ones that, above all else, can absolutely cripple you if you are unaware of them and how they work in your particular case.

Power

There is a third influencer on how things are perceived. This is power – who has it, or who is perceived to have it.

It is important to understand both where the power actually lies in your own organisation and where people perceive it to lie. This is also true of the external environment in which you are operating.

There is a three-dimensional view of power:
1. The power to force someone to do something.
2. The power to influence what someone does.
3. The power to shape what someone wants to do in the first place.

The first is the most obvious power of leadership. Leaders can insist that individuals carry out certain tasks. This is generally the power of authority.

The second is the less obvious form. Certainly the person/people at the top of an organisation can influence how people behave, but actually a lot of that influence will come from their immediate managers or their peer group. This is also the power that is used most effectively in lobbying for change in the external environment.

The third form of power rarely comes directly from the top. It is more often immediately influenced by peer groups, who, after all, are those people with whom we have the strongest relationships and who are the ones we are more likely to trust.

I have taken this principle slightly further and identified some types of power, which I call 'power profiles', that I believe reside in organisations and have an impact on how effective the organisation can be.

- **Personal power:** This is the power of personality. Some might call this charisma. It is the power of the individual who has, or appears to have, a lot of self-confidence.
- **Status power:** This is essentially the power of position, where the individual is perceived to have high status within the organisation's hierarchical structure.
- **Resource power:** This is the power over money and the equipment, who has it and who can make decisions about where it goes.
- **Influencer power:** This is the power to influence how people think about a particular circumstance, person or set of people – often your political journalist.
- **Expert power:** This is the power of the person who is seen as having all the knowledge or information about a particular subject.
- **Popular power:** This is the power of the person who is well liked by others in the organisation and whose view will be listened to because individuals wish to be liked by this individual or be part of their gang.

All the above sorts of power lie with different individuals in the organisation and it is important you recognise who they are so that you can ensure that you are influencing these power sources yourself.

This may sound a little Machiavellian; however, actually it is simply common sense. When you are thinking about how to move the organisation forward and take your people with you, take the time to communicate with those individuals who can, by dint of their power profile, help you deliver the message.

Formal communication processes

We have already talked about the need for the chief executive and senior staff to be visible informally. It is also important to be visible formally. This means that you should regularly speak directly with staff in a formal fashion.

In small organisations (say less than 100 people) this is relatively easy to do.

In larger organisations, especially those that are regionally spread, it's a little harder and you need to be slightly more creative in how you make sure you are seen by your people. However, you could do things like attend a different region's meeting each month and give a piece of information about what is going on.

It is important to have some formal mechanisms because people only tend to invent information to fill in the gaps if they are not given the correct information in the first place.

Internal communication systems and structures

You need to ensure that your people (staff and volunteers) understand what is going on both inside and outside the organisation and that they know if there is any action they are required to take.

There are a number of communication mechanisms that are available to your organisation. Some are more appropriate than others and some work best depending upon the current circumstances. As a bare minimum I recommend that you have the following:

- All managers have monthly one-to-ones with their individual team members.
- A monthly briefing mechanism to share information about the state of the organisation.
- A staff forum or representative group for your staff (if you're not unionised).
- A whole organisation gathering once a year if possible (obviously for huge organisations this isn't usually possible – but some kind of cross-departmental gatherings when you can).

There is an old saying that 's/he who communicates leads'. What this means is that if you are the source of information it tends to reinforce you as someone with power and authority. So if you want your managers to be seen as leaders within your organisation you need to allow them to do most of the direct communication with their teams. If you are the one who consistently gives the information to members of staff, or indeed consults with the staff, it makes it easier for them to disregard their line manager. So, no matter what the temptation is to deliver communication yourself, don't do it! Part of your managers' role is to communicate. Let them.

I shall talk about consultation separately. For the moment I want to focus on the delivery of information to your staff, volunteers and others.

Your communication structure will depend to a large extent on the size of your organisation and the size of your management/leadership team. Nonetheless, there are some basic rules which should stand fast regardless of how large or small your organisation is.

Rules of effective communication structures

- Staff need to know what information they can expect to receive and at what time/date, and that it is a regular repeating occurrence.
- Managers need to know what information is to be communicated and what is not – in particular what the key messages are that need to be put across.
- Staff need to be given information in a context that is relevant to them.

In my experience the following basic structure seems to work best in terms of ensuring that the right information is disseminated at the right time. This is based on a concept called 'team briefing', which is a cascade mechanism that you may already be familiar with.

Team briefing – the provision of information

STAGE 1

Senior team meeting
- Once a month agree what the messages are that need to be communicated to staff.
- Make sure you always link the core messages to the vision and your beneficiaries – after all, that's what you exist for.
- Agree both the facts that need to be communicated and the management line associated with those facts.
- A useful structure is around the four Ps:
  1. **Progress:** How well is the organisation/ department doing, what has it achieved, etc.?
  2. **Policy:** What new policies/procedures/ systems, etc. do people need to know about?
  3. **People:** What information is there about, for instance, new members of staff, clients, service users and beneficiaries?
  4. **Points for action:** As a result of the first three Ps what are staff, volunteers and others required to do?

Jane Gurney, the CEO of Essex and Herts Air Ambulance Trust, adds a further P which stands for 'Patients'. Every month part of their briefing includes an update on patients who have been rescued by the air ambulance, progress on their recovery, thanks yous, happy endings and stories. I think it's a great idea and her team members love it.

Note that in stage 1 you are not just agreeing the facts that need to be communicated, but also the management line. In other words, how is the message to be communicated and what behaviours do managers need to engage in during the communication in order to support the line? It is *critical* that you clarify with your managers that they must brief all decisions as if they were their own. To put it simply, even if they disagreed in the meeting with a course of action, outside the meeting they have to act and behave positively about that course of action. Be clear that it is not acceptable for managers to say things like 'well, I don't agree with it either' or 'don't blame me, it wasn't my decision'. Make it clear that managers have absolute freedom to challenge and argue during the meeting or with you privately. But, once the decision has been taken, they must support it, otherwise it undermines not just that particular decision but also the whole of the leadership team.

If, having worked with them on the rationale for the decision/action, they still can't take the management line then you will need to have a long and hard conversation with them about their future as a manager in the organisation. You simply cannot afford to have your managers undermining decisions and actions. It is completely unfair on staff and volunteers. This can be hard to do, but don't shirk it. If they really can't adopt the line, then they have to go. This is why it is so important to ensure that you incorporate into the job description of your management team clear information about what it means to be a leader/manager in the organisation and what is expected of them.

STAGE 2

Managers prepare
- Translate the information gathered at the senior team meeting into something that is relevant to their team.
- Anticipate and think about likely questions to ensure managers can answer them or know how to handle them if not.

Managers must publicly support management decisions. If a manager feels unconfident about briefing a particular point or has such strong reservations that they are uncomfortable about supporting it publicly, then this is their opportunity to seek guidance and support from their own line manager. In stage 2, work with the managers initially to help them to make the information relevant to their teams. For instance, if the main item to be communicated to staff under 'progress of the organisation' on the core brief is that £50,000 has been donated towards a particular project, then the finance manager might talk about the impact on the bank balance, the project manager might discuss the impact on staff workloads and so on.

STAGE 3

Managers brief
- Managers meet with their teams and brief the four Ps, making it directly relevant to their team wherever possible.
- Brief core information as well as information that is 'local', i.e. relevant to that team only.
- Plan time for questions, comments and feedback.

As the CEO you should try to 'walk the job' during briefing a few times a year (see 'Walking the job' later in this chapter). Sitting quietly at the back and just listening gives you a good sense of how well your managers are briefing and what sorts of questions the teams ask. Plus it demonstrates that you take it seriously and that it matters.

STAGE 4

Feedback

- Managers communicate back up the line, either immediately or at the next senior team meeting, what the feedback/reaction has been, any questions that have been asked and so on.

You will need to ensure that your managers are sharing information appropriately and in the right way, so I strongly advocate some formal training. It is not always immediately obvious to people what is the best way of sharing information, and by being properly trained they are more likely to make a good job of it. This is critical in the context of the performance of the organisation. If people don't know what they need to know, they can't do what they need to do.

With the process I describe above I suggest that there are a couple of days between your senior management team meeting and the managers' briefing with their staff. This gives them plenty of time to prepare.

I also strongly suggest that you ask managers to brief their staff at the same time each month (so that staff know exactly when the meeting is and can organise their work to make sure there are no distractions) and at the same time as each other (so that new information is not passed between teams before they have heard from their own manager, otherwise it can get distorted).

Establish a staff forum

A staff forum is a way for staff to 'gossip' in a more structured way by having an agenda for the discussion which should enable those who disagree with the expressed view to speak up in a relatively safe environment. They will perceive the environment as safe because there are no managers there and they will be less likely to feel nervous about expressing their real opinion.

In my experience staff forums, particularly if they are run well and the right tone has been set at the beginning, are enormously beneficial to an organisation. To begin with, it is unwise to rely solely on feedback from your managers about how staff are in general or how they are receiving/reacting to information/changes and so on. This is not because your managers deliberately tell fibs. It is just that they will hear and report back on the things that matter to them, which may not be the same as the things that you believe to be important or, indeed, that the staff believe to be important. Secondly, human nature is such that we do find it very difficult to be entirely honest with our bosses. There are usually perfectly valid reasons for this: we want to look good; we want to impress our boss; we like them and can see they are under pressure, so don't want to add to it; we believe we can handle the problem/situation ourselves; and so on. Therefore, your managers' staff are likely not to be entirely honest with them, and your direct reports are, in turn, unlikely to be completely honest with you, even if you both think they are.

With a staff forum you get feedback directly from staff, without it being interpreted or managed by your middle/senior managers. Staff tend to feel more directly involved in the wider context of the organisation.

When we introduced the concept of staff forum into DSC, I asked the newly voted-in leader of the staff forum, Sarah Westlake, what she felt the benefits were. She came up with the following (her words are reproduced exactly).

- Encourages a free and easy flow of communication between staff.
- Encourages debate about processes on a shop-floor level.
- When the information gathered is used successfully and acted upon by senior management team it helps the staff feel listened to and that their opinions have worth and gravity.
- Really gets ideas moving on how to improve and work with each other, so is innovative.
- Helps staff realise what kind of pressures each team is under and can liaise to offer help on the ground.
- When senior management team sets aside time and covers the phones and so on to enable this to happen, it makes staff feel valued.

It is really important to make sure that the forum has agreed with you its terms of reference. Although the forum is for the staff you need to ensure that it doesn't descend into a whinge-fest or a virtual bullying forum where people think it's OK to bitch about their line managers or other colleagues.

And make sure you give training to the leaders of the forum. Our staff forum leaders at DSC are skilled in how to run the meetings; how to manage difficult conversations; how to give feedback to me appropriately; and how to communicate with other senior staff if issues have cropped up in the forum which need to be addressed.

Suggest to your staff that they might like to participate in a staff forum. Explain that it is not a management-controlled exercise, but an opportunity for them to gather together, without management present, to discuss their reactions to what is going on in the organisation and to come up with ideas, suggestions and feedback to the management. However, do make it absolutely clear that the forum is an *addition* to normal communication channels and not a replacement.

How to implement a staff forum

Encourage the staff to appoint a leader for the forum and then work hard with the leader to help them to understand things from the management perspective as well as from the staff one. That way, if they have access to information about what is going on and why they can discuss and share it with the rest of staff from a more informed perspective, the feedback you get will be constructive and helpful, even if occasionally painful!

I must stress again, however, that you need to be *absolutely* clear that the forum is an addition to normal communication channels with their manager and should not be used as a replacement. What you mustn't do is to rely primarily on the forum for your information, otherwise you undermine the ability of your managers to manage.

You cannot control the forum (and indeed, neither should you try), although what you can do is clarify what it is for and make it clear that the staff forum is not for personal attacks on colleagues or managers.

All-staff meetings

Staff away days have their place but too often we can fall into the trap of thinking that the business of team building and communication is polished off by getting everyone together once or twice and year and giving them an enjoyable experience.

This is not the case. Teams are built minute by minute, hour by hour, through the daily, weekly and monthly working and practices of your line managers and their teams.

Having said that, I think that it can be very useful to gather everyone together at least once a year. But I do believe that it has to be meaningful. While it might be good fun for people to hang out and play games, at the end of the day you need to ensure that the game playing is in some way genuinely contributing to everyday effectiveness or the long-term future of your organisation.

All-staff days are a good place to look at the working of the organisation as a whole – to ask people what is going well, what is going less well and what can be done about it. They are also a good way of getting other people to interact with one another. And, if your training budget isn't too tight, and the numbers warrant it, you can get everyone to experience some kind of standard training by asking a trainer to deliver a course for you in-house.

But on the whole, my experience tells me that the best use of this type of day is to get people thinking about the future and engaging with them in conversations about where the organisation is going and how it can get there.

For this kind of day to be really effective I think it is worth getting someone external to facilitate it for you. The reality is that you cannot facilitate your own organisation as well as someone from the outside can, because no matter how skilled you are, your audience (i.e. your staff/volunteers) are likely to perceive you as having some kind of hidden agenda (and indeed, you probably do, because you will have your own thoughts about the issues and ideas about what to do). They are more likely to perceive an external person as not having an agenda. This makes it easier for you to participate fully yourself and for them to be more open and participative.

However, this is not always possible, especially if money is tight. In that case, here are some simple ideas to help your all-staff day to be successful:

- Be clear about what you want the outcome of the day to be. Is it to inform, consult, train or something different?
- Make sure 80% of the day consists of people talking to each other or working together on something: avoid long, big plenary sessions where they have to sit and listen.
- Get their feedback on the day. What worked for them? What didn't? What would they like to see next year?

Don't forget – two important things

First: Staff are often more interested in how the organisation is seen or is doing in the external context than you realise. Don't focus internal communication solely on internal stuff. Give staff the chance to feel proud, excited, cross and engaged about the organisation in its external context. For instance, talk about policy, politics, the state of the economy and how it affects the organisation and your beneficiaries; get their views and ideas.

Second: Volunteers. Volunteers. Volunteers. You need to take as much care about communicating with them as you do with staff. Find an appropriate mechanism and make it work. And remember that for volunteers face-to-face communication is just as important as it is for staff. It's lazy to rely on written communication. And not only that – it doesn't work! If your volunteers are spread about, do shift work and so on, then find a way. There is one if you look hard enough. Even if it means you and/or your managers coming in one evening or weekend to talk to them. It's part of your responsibility. And they are very important!

Confidentiality

I am always deeply concerned about the notion of confidentiality at work. In my experience, I don't see how things can be confidential at work (unless it is about someone's personal life). What do I mean by that? Well, it's our job as leaders to lead and manage our organisation. So it's technically a dereliction of duty if you or any of your managers are given a piece of information about a member of staff, a piece of work or whatever that is detrimental to the effectiveness of the organisation and which you then fail to act upon.

You have to ask yourself, if someone is telling you something in confidence, what exactly is their motive here? Are they trying to get someone else into trouble? Trying to make you think badly of another individual? If people genuinely want a situation resolved then why is confidentiality needed? OK, it may be that they are afraid of being bullied if people find out what they have said, in which case you need to deal with it appropriately and sensitively and in line with your policies and procedures. But for the most part, I suspect that when people hide behind confidentiality it's because they want to stick the boot in without taking responsibility for it. Passing the buck to you to handle.

So I think this approach should be discouraged. Confidential and anonymous feedback encourages an atmosphere of back-stabbing. Our role as leaders is to help our staff behave like adults. That means helping them to own their problems and fix them themselves.

So how do you deal with it? Well, to begin with, if someone comes to you and says they want to tell you something in confidence you should say 'No'. That is, you can't listen to what they have to say in confidence because it is your responsibility as a leader to resolve issues within the organisation. Tell them that if an individual has a problem then you will help them to resolve it. That might involve coaching them so that they go and speak to the individual concerned, or you might step in. Ask people how they would feel if someone told them that another person had a problem with them. The first thing they would want to know is 'Who is this person?'. You can't change anything if you don't know exactly what the problem is and who has it.

You don't have to be brutal of course. You can be empathetic and compassionate while at the same time helping the individual to take ownership of their feedback.

I was doing some coaching in an organisation that had a recently appointed chief executive. At a meeting that I was observing the chair told the chief exec that 'some people' had 'some problems' with him. When I asked who had what problems she replied that she couldn't tell me or the chief exec because she had been told in confidence. I pointed out that if the chief exec didn't know who had what problem he could not reasonably be expected to deal with it and, therefore, the chair could not reasonably expect him to make a judgement about what, if anything, needed to change. So his best course of action was to simply ignore it. All that this anonymous, confidential feedback accomplished was to make the chief exec feel undermined and begin to lose confidence – with absolutely no chance of doing anything about it.

My view? Nine times out of ten, it's pure mischief-making or buck-passing. Grown-ups don't send anonymous messages! Don't fall into the trap of encouraging it by paying attention. Make it clear: I will help you to resolve the problem, or I will resolve it for you. If you choose not to resolve it yourself and don't want me to do anything about it either, then that's your choice. But don't expect me to take it seriously in that case and don't complain about it. If you do want me to intervene, then remember that I will not be able to keep your identity anonymous – because that is unfair on the individual being criticised. For goodness' sake, our own courts of law do not allow accusers to be anonymous to their accused. How is it that what is absolutely *not* acceptable in civil life is acceptable in work life, particularly when the issues are usually not that serious?

Having said that, you do of course need to bear in mind that bullying and harassment need to be treated somewhat differently (and make sure you have an up-to-date and workable policy to deal with this). In cases of this sort, you may have to be a little more flexible.

Walking the job

When you are at the top of the organisation it is extremely hard to be accessible to the vast majority of your staff, especially if you spend all your time in meetings or at your desk. This is why it is so essential to 'walk the job' – where you wander about your office/offices so that you can see and be seen. But many chief execs and senior people find this enormously difficult to do. Excuses tend to go something like this:

- They might think I have no work to do if I am just wandering around.
- I don't want to interrupt them at their work.
- I'm too busy.

- It doesn't make any difference to the staff whether I walk the job or not so long as they know I am doing my job.
- It's not a good use of my time.
- Staff will perceive it as meaningless.
- I don't feel confident enough.

The point is you need to be visible – literally.

Why walk the job? Because...
- Staff get used to seeing you around and so are likely to be less intimidated by your job title which leads to more open, spontaneous, honest conversations.
- You can observe things in action for yourself.
- You get the opportunity to ask questions.
- Staff have the chance to 'nobble' you if they have something they want to ask.
- Staff perceive that you are interested in them and their work.

Having said that, walking the job is one of the things that many chief execs tell me they find hardest to do. This is largely because they see it as apparently purposeless and they don't know what to talk about or to say to people. So here are some tips:
- Schedule walk-the-job time in your diary so that you don't forget to do it.
- Do it often, and then you will feel less uncomfortable and so will the staff.
- Smile and say a general good morning as you walk into the room.
- Look at charts/things on walls, especially if they are tracking progress and ask questions about them.
- Ask what they are working on at the moment.
- Ask what their priority is for the week, or what they thought about the information contained in the last staff briefing, or what their biggest challenge is.
- If you know something personal, for example, that they have just been on holiday, ask them how it was.
- If you come across something that needs action – then act on it. Show that you are paying attention.
- Try to listen more than you talk.
- Don't use it as an opportunity to tell someone off.
- Look for opportunities to catch people doing something right!

Consultation

> The greatest compliment that was ever paid me was when one asked me what *I thought*, and attended to my answer.
>
> Henry David Thoreau, 'Life Without Principle'

The above quote sums up for me one of the main benefits of consulting people. Not only is it useful, people feel good when you've done it. You are one brain with one way of looking at the world. Many brains mean many ideas and many ways of looking at the world. There is a very good chance that when you ask people what they think and what their ideas are you will hear things that you didn't expect: fresh ideas; new ways of looking at old problems.

Secondly, nothing makes people feel as valued and important as being asked for their opinions and ideas. It makes them feel part of something more than just their job and that they have the chance to contribute. That alone is likely to make them want to engage more in change and development in the organisation. Even if you can't act on what they suggest, at least you have asked them and they know that you have.

So you can see that consultation with staff and volunteers is vitally important, but is so often done badly. This is because we are not always clear what is and is not up for consultation, or indeed, even what consultation actually is.

Genuine consultation is that which begins *before* you have decided what action to take. That is, you ask people for their input, ideas, feedback and so on before you take any decisions.

There are five stages to consultation:
1. Consult on what the decision(s) should be.
2. Consider what you have heard before making the decision.
3. Make the decision.
4. Communicate the decision and ask for feedback on it if necessary.
5. Check that it is being implemented and is working, and amend the decision if appropriate.

Do not tell staff you are consulting them if you have already made up your mind. If you have already decided (and it is entirely right that occasionally you will make decisions without consulting) then make it clear that you are just informing them. If you *pretend* to consult and then don't act on their feedback your consultation mechanism will lose all credibility – and your ability to get people to implement your decisions will be undermined.

Generally speaking, when consulting on big decisions, it is better to conduct consultations face-to-face around a specific set of questions. For example, if you are consulting about the cramped conditions in the offices and are aware that an office move may be required then you might ask questions like:
- What is it about our current conditions that is causing us difficulty?
- What are the possible solutions to the problem?
- What haven't we considered?

This way, you may find that people come up with a solution that you hadn't even considered. And at the very least you will be able to say genuinely, when you brief your final decision, that you had listened to staff and taken into account their views. Then they are more likely to co-operate or even own the decision that has been taken. But it needs to be genuine. Believe it or not, staff really do have inbuilt bullshit detectors!

Listening

Talking about consultation (which obviously involves the ability to listen) brings me on to the issue of listening.

One of the key skills you need as a leader is the ability to listen. It's a funny thing when you think about it: when we are young we are taught how to read, how to write and how to speak – but no one actually teaches us how to listen.

I wanna be the leader
I wanna be the leader
Can I be the leader?
Can I? I can?
Promise? Promise?
Yippee I'm the leader
I'm the leader

OK what shall we do?

This poem by Roger McGough usually makes people laugh because our normal concept of leadership (especially at the top) is that the leader knows exactly what needs to be done and how, and, therefore, does the deciding. In this poem someone has begged to be the leader but doesn't know what to do.

But actually the poem, for me, is very telling about what really powerful leadership is about. It's about asking and listening first before deciding. So, 'Now what shall we do?' is a really good question for a leader to ask.

Those of you who have attended coaching or counselling skills courses will, no doubt, have experienced the training that distinguishes between active and passive listening. You will have learned that you need to indicate that you are listening through appropriate body language, using your voice to indicate listening through grunts and 'mmmms'. However, I suspect that if you have to think about doing those things in order to demonstrate that you are listening then you probably aren't genuinely listening at all.

Actually, I don't believe listening is a skill. I believe it's an attitude. When you genuinely want to hear what someone has to say you do pay close attention and listen carefully. So if you want to be an effective listener then the trick is to make yourself want to hear. What makes me want to listen is the fear that I might miss something really important if I don't!

Although, isn't it funny how people think you haven't listened if you haven't agreed? That is why, when you disagree with someone, you need to demonstrate you have listened by being clear about why you don't agree.

Listening is hard in the normal course of things because we have so much going on inside our heads. The trouble is that our thoughts don't switch off when we are listening: we are interpreting what we hear; comparing it with what we already know; thinking of a response. That is normal human behaviour. And in some ways I suspect it's even harder when you are at the top because you have access to so much information which can cause interference when you are listening to others.

Further, the way in which we listen is hugely affected by the filters through which we are hearing the speaker. We listen with the six Es: our ears, our eyes, our emotions, our experience, our expectations and our egos. Obviously we hear what people have to say, and not just through their words but also the tone of their voice. We hear with our **eyes**, in that we observe their body language and thereby add interpretation to the words we are hearing. We also hear with our **emotions**. If we are feeling negative or cross then that is likely to affect our listening. We have **experiences** which affect how we hear: we may have a previous, negative experience of an individual which makes it harder for us to listen openly, or we may feel we've heard it all before. We have **expectations**: we will anticipate what someone is going to say and how they are going to say it because of who they are, or our past experience of them, or what we assume that *type* of person or person at that job level is likely to say. And finally we listen with our **egos**. We listen for what makes us feel good about ourselves, or shows us in a good light.

This is how people will be listening to you all the time. There are only two things that you can do to counteract it. Firstly, recognise that this is what's happening and adjust your speaking accordingly. Secondly, ensure that other people's experience of your listening tells them you are open to hearing them, because that is more likely to encourage similar listening in them.

In terms of your own listening, focus on your attitude and approach to your listening. I do not believe it is possible to listen in a vacuum, to have absolutely no thoughts or reaction to what you are hearing. So I believe the best approach is to focus on your attitude to your listening. Are you:

- Listening **for being right**, i.e. right about them or right about your view?
- Listening **for punishing**, i.e. looking for the mistake or them proving to you how useless they are?
- Listening **for proving you know best**?
- Listening **for making your point**?
- Listening **for telling your story**?
- Listening **for them being wrong**?

The type of listening that will make us more effective as leaders is:

- Listening **for understanding:** where are they coming from? Why are they saying what they are saying?
- Listening **for resolution:** what can you do to move things forward?
- Listening **for action:** what can you do to help?
- Listening **for possibility:** what new idea is coming out of their words?
- Listening **for resolving breakdowns:** where can you find agreement?
- Listening **for building relationships:** where is the common ground?

You won't always listen well. None of us do. But at the very least you can continually ask yourself: are you listening with the right attitude?

Some critical dos and don'ts!

DO

- Have an ear to the gossip
- Communicate primarily through your managers
- Communicate frequently and regularly with staff and volunteers
- Genuinely consult
- Manage your own behaviour

DON'T

- Gossip yourself
- Assume managers will communicate effectively without training and discussion
- Rely on all-staff/volunteer days to communicate and inspire
- Consult if you have no intention of changing your mind
- Allow the way you come across to interfere with what you are actually trying to do

5 Top teams

If anything goes bad, I did it. If anything goes semi-good, we did it. If anything goes really good, you did it. That's all it takes to get people to win football games for you.
Attributed to Paul 'Bear' Bryant,
American college football player and coach

Outcomes
After reading this chapter you will:
- Know how to get your top team to behave more 'corporately'
- Understand some of the underlying dynamics that influence their behaviour
- Have some tips and ideas about how to help them to be a successful top team

What exactly is a top team?

Of all of the complaints, worries and problems that I encounter from listening to and working with chief execs in the sector, the issue of the effectiveness of the top team is right there at the top of the list.

And you can see why. You simply cannot do your job alone. You need a top team around you who act corporately, who work well together, who debate and discuss robustly, but who also know when to shut up and get on with it. These are the people who have a can-do attitude and take responsibility and ownership not just of their bit but of the whole organisation.

Whatever the size of your organisation, your top team is absolutely critical in helping you to achieve the organisation's vision, mission and objectives. A poorly performing top team means a poorly performing organisation.

But I wonder. I wonder how much of what you get is what you asked for?

Have you made it clear to everyone in the team how incredibly important they are? Have you pointed out to them that *they* are the team that works with you to provide direction and leadership for the whole organisation? That it is this team that needs to embody the values and culture of the organisation? They need to know that this is the team which creates the environment that people work in, that has an impact on how staff feel about the organisation, that generates the trust in the leadership and direction of the organisation, and, ultimately, that enables the organisation to deliver the results that you need.

You know already that a weak link in this team is extremely damaging and limits your ability to achieve your goals. Firstly, a member of the top team who is working counter to the rest of the team damages trust in the whole leadership of the organisation, which in turn gives rise to credibility issues for the whole team. Secondly, what they do and say reflects on you. People are more inclined to believe those people who are closer to them in 'rank' (for want of a better word) than those who appear far away – so no matter what you say and do yourself, if your message is not being carried down by the rest of your top team then it will not be delivered or believed.

I have noticed that in many organisations the top team is not a top team at all but simply a reporting mechanism. They provide information about progress and results, but do not really engage in a mutual and dynamic conversation about the organisation as a whole, in particular where it is going and how it is going to get there.

Richard Hackman defines a real team as one that has 'a collective task that demands a high level of interdependency among its members, something that can only be accomplished together; and clear and stable boundaries so that membership is not constantly changing, and it is easy to tell who is on the team'.

How effective is your top team?

How do you establish what the issues are in your team? How do you know if the team is working well together or not?

Since 1998 the Hay Group has worked in partnership with Harvard University and Dartmouth College. They conducted a study which concluded that the main reason top teams fail is because of the behaviour and actions of the chief executive.

The study looked at how the leadership/managerial style of the chief executive had an impact on the ability of the top team to perform. They looked at six dominant leadership styles and assessed that style against the subsequent performance of the team. The styles are:

- **Coercive:** highly directive, forcing people to do things, not involving people in decision-making and so on.
- **Authoritative:** consulting and listening, but providing clear direction and decisive in action.
- **Affiliative:** involving everyone and focusing on relationships and camaraderie.
- **Democratic:** essentially voting, i.e. going with the group majority vote.
- **Pace-setting:** fast moving, focus on action and results.
- **Coaching:** minimal direction, getting people to set their own agendas.

They discovered that in order of effectiveness, in terms of performance of the top team, the styles rank as follows:

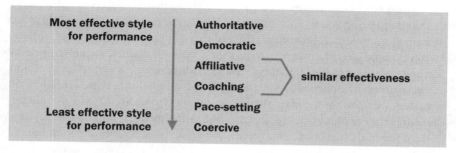

Do you think you are being authoritative when in fact you are being coercive? Are you sure that what you see as being democratic is not simply ducking out of making hard decisions?

I want to pick on this word 'democratic'. And I want to be clear. Voluntary organisations are not democracies. Let me say it again – not democracies. A democracy is one where people vote in their leaders. You didn't get voted in. You were appointed by a board. The same is true for your senior team. You appointed them (or your predecessor did). You cannot run your top team by getting people to vote. That's not to say that you shouldn't involve them, listen to them hard and sometimes do it their way or the majority way – but only because for a particular decision at a particular time that is the right way.

It's important not to completely polarise these styles of leading your top team. In the real world, you usually need a combination of them, and the trick is to ensure that you are using the right style at the right time. For example, there will be a time when you need to set the pace – when the need for change is urgent. But constantly operating at full pelt will eventually wear people out. There will be a time when you have to insist that a certain line is taken or that a decision goes a certain way, because the future of the organisation depends on it. But again, this should be rare. The trick is to be aware of what your natural inclination is and ensure that you are actively thinking about what style is appropriate in what circumstances. And if you find that the style you are using is not working – then use a different style. But don't get stuck in only one way of operating.

How do you know if your team is performing?

If your top team is performing well, in addition to seeing results you will also see demonstrated the following behaviours:

- flexibility;
- establishing and meeting standards;
- co-operation;
- empathy;
- commitment;
- energy.

The following questionnaire can be a helpful starting point for establishing where your team is doing well, and where you need to concentrate your efforts. If the team scores low on one statement, it may be that you need to spend some time and attention there. This questionnaire can be completed by you alone, or by your team together. I use a variation of this a couple of times a year with my own top team. We all complete it and then we look at each statement one by one and share our scores. If there is either a wide discrepancy between members of the team on one particular statement, or if overwhelmingly we score low on one, then we open up the statement for discussion and discuss why people put the scores they did and what we can do about moving the scores upwards.

Generally this works extremely well, particularly as it gives the members of the team an opportunity to raise issues in a non-threatening manner, given that it's in the context of a more general conversation.

You can, of course, reproduce this self-assessment questionnaire and change the statements to ones that feel more relevant to your organisation. This one is generalised to illustrate the example, and the statements are ones that I have discovered reflect common issues at top-team level.

High-performing top teams

Self-assessment: how well do the following statements describe you/ your team?

1 Has a common understanding of the vision/mission/purpose

Low				Medium					High
1	2	3	4	5	6	7	8	9	10

2 Sees itself as accountable for the whole

Low				Medium					High
1	2	3	4	5	6	7	8	9	10

3 Constantly seeks to improve the organisation

Low				Medium					High
1	2	3	4	5	6	7	8	9	10

4 Focuses on solutions not problems

Low				Medium					High
1	2	3	4	5	6	7	8	9	10

5 Engages in robust and useful debate

Low				Medium					High
1	2	3	4	5	6	7	8	9	10

6 Focuses on strategic and high-level operational issues

Low				Medium					High
1	2	3	4	5	6	7	8	9	10

7 Publicly shows a united front

Low				Medium				High
1	2	3	4	5	6	7	8	9	10

8 Has a high level of empathy and co-operation with one another

Low				Medium				High
1	2	3	4	5	6	7	8	9	10

9 Communicates openly, honestly and appropriately with one another

Low				Medium				High
1	2	3	4	5	6	7	8	9	10

10 Demonstrates trust and loyalty to all fellow members of the leadership team

Low				Medium				High
1	2	3	4	5	6	7	8	9	10

What is the top team's scope and purpose?

The purpose of the top team is to create the conditions for success in future. They do this in two ways: through their 'technical' responsibilities and through their leadership responsibilities.

A member of a top team essentially has two parts to their role, each of which is of equal importance (but interestingly, only one of which is usually monitored!). One is their 'technical' accountability, for example the head of finance is accountable for the finance function, the director of operations is accountable for the operations function, the director of policy is accountable for policy development and so on. The other part of their role is as a leader of the whole organisation. Staff generally do see the top team as being accountable for the whole, even when the team doesn't always behave in that way.

One of the major breakdowns at a top level, in my experience, is where the members of the top team have not realised about their wider responsibilities in the corporate context and therefore tend to operate in their own silo, that is, focusing on the work of their own bit of the organisation and not taking responsibility for the whole. And yet, this is why they are a member of a top team – precisely because, at their level, delivery in their area is about the contribution to the whole.

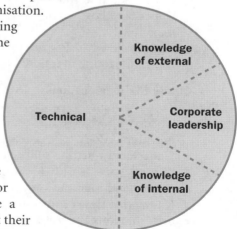

The top-team role

Many chief executives find this a real problem at top-team level. And often actually the cause of the problem is very simple: no one (the no one being you – the chief exec!) has explained this part of their responsibility to the members of the top team. There are some who grasp it naturally – but not many – and, therefore, if you are a chief executive, it is important that you ensure that your top team understands the entirety of their role – not just the half of it that relates to delivery in their specific area. You can't expect them simply to learn this other part by osmosis, mainly because, in fact, it is the hardest part of the job. It needs to be spelled out, monitored, appropriate behaviour rewarded and inappropriate behaviour dealt with.

Clarifying the top team's technical responsibilities is generally very straightforward – members need to deliver on their bit of the organisation's work.

Their leadership responsibilities are a little harder to explain. Simply put, they are usually something like this:

- To participate in robust discussion with the rest of the senior team about the long-term future of the organisation.
- To create a culture in the organisation that is compatible with its ethos and vision.
- To own the leadership message and act as if it was theirs.
- To be accountable for the overall performance of the organisation.

How do you achieve their understanding and commitment?

Clarify the context

Does your team:

- Understand and commit to the vision, mission and purpose of the organisation?
- Understand how they fit into the wider context?
- Understand how other members of the team fit into the wider context?
- Understand how the direction and plans for the organisation will deliver the results?
- Understand what they need to do in their technical area in order to contribute to the overall results?

Clarify the expectations

Does your team:

- Understand what is expected of them as someone at the top of the organisation?
- Understand what the culture is that you are trying to create, and buy into it?
- Understand what the leadership line is of your particular organisation?
- Know what the priorities are?
- Seek solutions and not over-analyse problems?

Clarify the behaviours
Does your team:
- Understand the decision-making process?
- Understand the limits of their authority?
- Understand what are considered appropriate leadership behaviours?
- Hold one another accountable for meeting commitments and deadlines?
- Know how to communicate effectively with one another?

Conditions for success
I have observed that really great top teams appear to have the following things in common.
1. There is a clear compelling direction.
2. The structure is appropriate to the needs of the organisation.
3. The right people are in the right jobs.
4. They are supported by their chief exec and trustees.
5. They are continually developing.

So how do you make sure these ingredients are in place?

Establish a clear compelling direction
This sounds self-evident, but does your team really understand the overall direction of the organisation?
- Don't assume they know the direction.
- Articulate it for them.
- If you can't get agreement, get alignment.

Get the structure right
This is not so much the organisational structure, but the structure of communication and responsibility within the team itself:
- Establish norms and enforce them.
- Create guidelines for how your top-team meetings are run.
- Establish how you expect people to interact with one another.
- Clarify the decision-making structure and ensure that at any decision point, it is clear what the actual decision is about, what kind of decision it is (i.e. consensus, collegiate or consulted) and who is going to take it.

Get the right people
Easier said than done! And very often you inherit people who you have to work with. Nonetheless, if the people you inherit aren't working with you then you have to surround yourself with people who are. Not 'yes' men or women. But people who are enthusiastic, engaged and who challenge you even as they're working alongside you.

Here my advice is, given a choice between those people who are highly technically competent and those people who have the right *attitude*, I would tend to choose the latter. This is because it is relatively easy to train people in the skills and knowledge they need to do the job; it is almost impossible to train people in the right attitude.

Look for someone who:
- has a high degree of emotional intelligence;
- has enthusiasm and energy for the job;
- demonstrates empathy for others;
- demonstrates integrity;
- has the ability to challenge the team to live up to its values;
- has the ability to engage in productive conflict;
- openly says what they are thinking;
- 'walks the talk', i.e. matches behaviour to words;
- can speak for those who are not present without putting their own particular spin on it.

Support them

What does this actually mean? Well, I think it's about:
- allowing them to make mistakes without getting it in the neck;
- talking through with them what they are doing – but allowing them to make their own decisions;
- backing them up when they get it wrong;
- praising them publicly when they get it right.

Develop them

Don't assume that they know how to do all the things that are expected of them at the top of the organisation. If you don't want them to learn the hard way (and make life difficult for you and their people along the way!) you must ensure that they participate in learning and development activities such as:
- facilitated planning days;
- leadership training;
- work shadowing;
- having a dedicated coach (a professionally qualified one who you pay for).

Group dynamics

You need to have a basic understanding of what is going on at the group-dynamic level in order to be able to know how to deal appropriately with some of the (frankly often bizarre!) behaviour you see at the top of the organisation.

It is my observation that the nearer people get to the top, the more often you see examples of childlike (even childish) behaviour. Why is this?

Well, if you think about the standard model of an organisation in the voluntary sector it probably looks something like this:

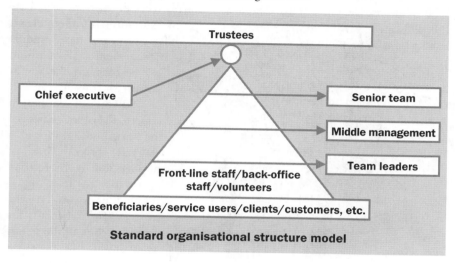

Standard organisational structure model

You may have more or fewer layers in between you and the front-line staff, but essentially there is a clear linear structure. Now, if you turn that structure around to represent what really happens in an organisation in terms of the weight of responsibility it looks something like this:

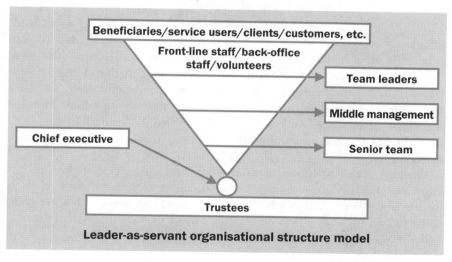

Leader-as-servant organisational structure model

(Incidentally, this reverse organisational model I call the 'leader-as-servant' model. It is supposed to demonstrate that our role as leaders is to support the rest of the organisation so that they can serve our service-users/beneficiaries, rather than the other way around. It is a powerful model and I think very effective – why not share the concept with your team?)

In this model you can see that service users/beneficiaries and so on have a broad base of support. This starts with the front-line/back-office staff and volunteers, who in turn have a base of support in their team leaders, who have middle management – all of whom are leaning on the senior team for support.

So you can see that, in fact, all other parts of the organisation have a relatively broad base of support, that is, more than one person to lean on – including you, as you have the trustees (theoretically!) for support. But all the senior team has is one person – you. If you can visualise them literally standing on you, you might get a picture of how unstable and insecure it can feel. One member of your team may feel they have both feet firmly planted in the middle of your back – they feel secure, stable and supported by you. But that doesn't leave a lot of room for the others. There may be one who, metaphorically speaking, feels they are balancing precariously on the heel of your right foot! They feel unstable and insecure. And being human beings, if they feel unstable and insecure, some way or another that is going to manifest itself in their behaviour.

On top of this, the level of expectation of them is very high. They are conscious that they are at the top, and, particularly for those who are relatively inexperienced, they suddenly have the horrible realisation that they are going to be judged by what others do (i.e. the people in their teams/departments) and not by what they as individuals do. That's a hard place to be.

So how does this manifest itself in your team and, more importantly, how on earth do you deal with it?

Managing group dynamics

There is a body of research which indicates that when a group of people get together, there is an unconscious pressure on them to conform to those perceived as powerful within the group. This power may come from the influence of an individual (i.e. someone seen as being more credible, charismatic, capable, more experienced, etc. than someone else) or the power of the majority. Not all members of the group will conform, but the critical point for you is that once the majority gang up it is more difficult for them to evaluate objectively or to consider the contrary evidence, namely that evidence which does not support the group's view. This is dangerous, because the fact is that the most powerful individual is often not right. And the majority view is not always the right view – simply the most commonly held one. There's also the risk of members of the team who *don't* give in to the group pressure feeling isolated.

To resolve this problem try the following:

- Clarify the task: what exactly is it we are trying to achieve? Discuss consequences and risks, and look at alternative routes – especially if everyone agrees!
- Clarify the group structure: accountabilities and authorities. If, for example, the director of fundraising wants to take a particular fundraising strategy route which the rest of the team does not support, you will be able to emphasise to the team that it is, nonetheless, the decision of the director of fundraising even if the rest of the team members do not agree – and that it is their job to support that individual.
- Allow individuals to express their differences openly, without allowing one particular position to be seen to be rewarded by you agreeing with it. Let everyone air their views before you come down on any one side.
- Acknowledge the need for social approval by complimenting people on their thinking, thanking them for their inputs and so on.
- Establish agreements by asking individuals to verbalise their thoughts – don't allow one person or small group to dominate. Take every person in turn and ask them what they think.
- Identify and illuminate in-groups and out-groups: point out openly where you see 'gangs' or cliques forming or where you see that one particular view is not gaining an appropriate hearing. Be honest (and, if possible, humorous) about it.

Human beings are gregarious folk who want to find people that they can identify with and perceive as sharing their values. They essentially seek other people who are like themselves.

In any organisation there are in-groups and out-groups which share common characteristics. This is normal, but creates the possibility that an entire group could be discredited or discounted because they are not part of the in-group. For example, a classic divide in the voluntary sector is between those in fundraising and those in finance: both teams stereotype and label the others, and have a perception and expectation of the behaviours in the other group, which they subsequently actively seek evidence to support.

To resolve this issue try the following:
- Illuminate the group stereotype: expose it and discuss it.
- Challenge the stereotypes: seek contrary evidence.
- Acknowledge, encourage and praise differences in opinion/approach.
- Accept and understand the need people have to identify with a group – but encourage open discussion.
- Base questions along the lines of:
  1. Tell me more about...?
  2. What do you think about...?
  3. How do you feel about...?
  4. What will you accept as evidence?
  5. What information are we missing?
  6. What counterarguments can you think of?
  7. What are the pros/cons?
  8. What are the consequences if we do...if we don't...?

People's willingness to adopt certain positions or support certain decisions will be highly influenced by what they perceive to be in- and out-groups, whether they perceive those groups to be like or unlike them, and where they see themselves in relation to those groups.

A simple analogy is that of a group of people, men and women, some of whom are parents and some of whom aren't. Within that group there will be mothers – who are likely to perceive all other mothers as being similar to themselves, so they are likely to feel the need to have common agreement with their similar in-group. Fathers will perceive themselves as being in the in-group (because they have the common bond of children) but dissimilar to it (because they are a different sex). The out-group will be those people who are not parents. The similar out-group will be women who are not parents (who share a sex, hence the perception of similarity, but not the role of parent – therefore, not in the in-group) and the dissimilar out-group will be men who are not parents (who are a different sex and are not parents so will see nothing in common between them and the in-group).

If the similar in-group of mothers is the 'lead' or most dominant force then you are likely to find that most of the other mothers will support that group view, that the fathers are more likely to go along with the group norm than the female non-parents who, nonetheless, may go along with the group because they can see some similarities between them and the in-group, even though they are not part of it. And the male non-parents are highly unlikely to conform to the norm of the female parents (mothers) because they perceive they have nothing in common.

Critically, this means that people will evaluate the *source* of a piece of information as being of more importance than the information itself. If it comes from a member of a similar in-group it will be given more validity by those members of that in-group than if it comes from a group perceived as dissimilar and out.

This is illustrated in the following diagram.

The point here is that you don't want decisions or positions to be influenced primarily by this in- and out-group dynamic – you want them to be influenced by the facts of the matter. To resolve this try the following:

- Focus discussions on outcomes, not method: what is it we are trying to achieve?
- Question discrepancies between original individual judgements and movement: highlight where people have changed their minds or view points and get them to elaborate on their thinking or where they haven't changed their mind and ask why not.
- Agree values around how information will be received and evaluated: so, for example, stress that we listen to all the facts/information before commenting or forming a view and that we then look at the pros and cons of all the information we're evaluating.
- Seek contrary evidence: anything that contradicts what we all think to test the validity and robustness of our thinking.
- Take into account out-group views: ensure that they get plenty of 'air-space'.

Subconscious group behaviours

Essentially, as adults we demonstrate behaviours which we learned as children in constructing defences to deal with subconscious anxiety – anxiety that we are not necessarily aware that we are feeling.

There are three classic 'symptoms' (for want of a better word) of this anxiety-avoidance pressure.

- Denial: not acknowledging our own feelings and often projecting these feelings onto others.
- Projection: benign and malign (that is heroising or demonising others). ·
- Scapegoating: group projection onto an individual.

I observed a real instance of these subconscious processes in action. I worked with an organisation that went through an intensive and extreme restructure. They began with around 40 members of the senior team (it was a large organisation). The new structure had only 20 senior team roles. So, consequently, half of the members of the previous senior team were either effectively demoted or made redundant. The other half of the team members were given brand new roles. In this process, a more junior member of staff was unexpectedly (to her and the rest of the senior team) promoted to one of the new senior roles (let's call her Grace). So she was new to the team and to the level of responsibility – and she was *the only one* in this situation. For the other members of the new team, they already had experience at that level, they all knew each other and, further, they were (naturally) very attached to their colleagues who had not 'made the grade', so to speak.

As a result of all of this, Grace entered a team of highly emotionally charged people who were feeling a curious mixture of guilt, sorrow and shame because they were 'in' and the others were 'out', but who also felt pride and excitement in their new roles and wanted to demonstrate that they were a good and right choice in the new structure.

Grace was naïve and completely oblivious to these feelings and leapt in full of enthusiasm, energy and ideas, combined with inexperience and a skewed understanding of what leadership was about at that level.

The team members were unable to deal with their feelings of anxiety and this was not acknowledged or dealt with by the leadership of the organisation. There was no time given to grieve and no guidance provided on how to deal with these conflicting and difficult emotions, either to the team members themselves or to Grace. The organisation, again, understandably, wanted the new team to just get on with the job. So these feelings remained unresolved.

The result was that Grace was effectively scapegoated. For a period of at least a year, her ideas were dismissed, her credibility was questioned, her skills were denigrated (or at least that's how it felt to her and I could see from observing that some of this was indeed happening – although perhaps not to the extreme that she perceived it). It was clear to me that what was happening was a classic example of group psychodynamic defence mechanisms: a combination of denial, projection and scapegoating enabled the team to function, if not wonderfully, at least enough to survive.

This story, while true, is probably an extreme example of these processes in action. Nonetheless, they may well be in action in your own team, so it is worth observing what is happening within it.

To resolve issues of this kind try to:
- encourage and allow the group to express anxiety;
- challenge individuals who 'speak on behalf of...' or use the term 'people';
- ask direct questions: 'How do you personally feel?';
- ask for the source of the feeling/perception;
- evaluate the evidence;
- establish a set of agreed values and associated behaviours – review them regularly.

How do you get the team to think and act corporately?

Getting your team to think and act 'corporately' is indeed a challenge. I would begin by agreeing with the team a set of guidelines to which you all sign up.

Get it written down and then get into the habit of reviewing how well you are doing against these values on a regular basis. At DSC, we regularly revisit these values and standards – in fact, it is usually the first item on every senior management team meeting agenda.

One of the mechanisms you have for working with your senior team is your regular meeting. You will determine what 'regular' is depending on the size of your organisation. But it is important that these meetings are diarised and the time, date and place of this meeting should be scheduled a whole year in advance, so that the team knows when it is and can organise its work around it.

Also, beware of the meeting simply being a catch-up or reporting mechanism. The bulk of this meeting probably ought to be focused on the future.

Have a properly set out agenda, prepared in advance, which makes it clear who is expected to speak on what topic, at what length and with what expected outcome. Then stick to it!

At your meeting make sure that you have clearly stated on the agenda, and also clarify at the start of each agenda item, the following:

- The expected outcome of discussion:
    1. Information?
    2. Decision?
    3. Consultation?
- What type of decision it is:
    1. Consensus: the majority.
    2. Collegiate: building it together.
    3. Owned: an individual.

And at the end of each agenda item or the meeting as a whole clarify what the management line will be, namely that we are all behind this decision in public, even if we disagreed privately. And make it clear that you will not tolerate your senior team ignoring the management line.

Managing team conflicts

You need to recognise that disagreement is an essential part of teamwork. If a team does not have strong feelings and emotions but relies simply on facts to make its decisions, it is effectively a less intelligent team (see Daniel Goleman's excellent work on emotional intelligence for more about this). The best decision-makers use both facts and feelings.

To begin with, unproductive conflict usually happens because it has not been made clear what the decision-making process is and who is responsible for specific decisions.

You need to clarify the distinction between responsibility, authority and accountability. Responsibility is for us all. We are responsible for the whole whether it is in our area or not. Authority is for the specific manager: who has the authority to make decisions about their bit of the business and at what level. And accountability is for their specific job and area. They are accountable for ensuring that their bit delivers.

Once that's cleared up you then need to make sure that people understand what type of decision is being made. Is it consensus (we all have to agree), owned (only the decision of the accountable person) or collegiate (worked out together)? All three of these decision-making strategies are acceptable. The trick is to know which one you need.

Be clear on these questions:
■ Whose decision is it?
■ At what point can the challenge stop?
■ What do you do if you really disagree with the decision and can't support it?
■ What are you looking for – agreement, alignment, acceptance?

My experience is that it is better to seek alignment than acceptance. If you ask someone to accept a decision that they don't agree with, you are effectively asking them to admit that they are wrong – and that is very hard to do, especially if they don't believe they are. If you ask them to align with it, you are making the point that you have heard that they don't agree, but that in the interests of moving forward can they position themselves behind the decision and support its implementation? Much easier for people to do!

If, however, conflict is still rearing its head and you are finding it hard to manage, you could try some of the following actions:

Build a positive approach
■ Explain that conflict is normal.
■ Encourage the team to understand that conflict is healthy if handled well.
■ Don't try to stifle or control disagreement: concentrate on encouraging individuals to listen to others' points of view.

Clarify expectations
■ Is the team clear about what its purpose is?
■ Do you have ground rules governing behaviours?
■ Have you talked about how to depersonalise conflict?
■ Is everyone clear about the level of authority/decision-making/ accountability of others within the team?
■ Do you have a structured way of dealing with discussions?
■ Are performance expectations clearly defined and understood by everyone?

Identify the type of conflict

- Is it personal to the individual?
- Is it conflict between individuals?
- Is it conflict with the whole team?
- Is it conflict between several individuals?
- Is it conflict with someone or a group outside the team?

Identify the team needs

- Situation: what is the problem to be solved?
- Options: what are the possible solutions?
- Long-term consequences: what would resolve the problem?
- Victory: what would a positive result look like?
- Execute: carry out the actions required.

Depersonalise the conflict

Create the environment for a solution by getting the team to address the following:

- What happened/is happening?
- What were/are the consequences (facts and feelings)?
- What would/will it take to move on?

Structure the discussion

- Let each person have their say.
- Engage neutral team members to reflect on areas of agreement and disagreement.
- Explore areas of disagreement to identify specific issues.
- Have opponents suggest modifications to their own points of view as well as to those of others.
- If you can't get agreement, go for alignment.

Key questions for resolving conflict

- What are we trying to accomplish as a team?
- What are each of our roles and responsibilities in accomplishing our goals?
- Do we have the 'who', 'when' and 'what' information?
- If we get into trouble who can help us?
- How will we arrive at decisions?
- What strengths do we bring to establishing our goals?
- How do we make ourselves more accessible to each other?
- What are we doing that is blocking resolution to this problem?
- How can we express differences without blaming others?
- What behaviours are unproductive? How can we help individuals to take ownership of their behaviour? Don't excuse a team member when they behave badly.

Some critical dos and don'ts!

DO

- Make sure the members of your top team understand their wider leadership responsibilities
- Be aware of the group dynamics underlying their behaviour
- Agree a set of leadership standards
- Have regular diarised meetings
- Allow healthy conflict to manifest itself

DON'T

- Try to take their decisions for them
- Forget how vulnerable they feel
- Forget to hold them to the standards
- Focus on the operation at the expense of the strategy
- Forget to clarify whose decision it is

6 Trusting trustees

There are two kinds of people, those who do the work and those who take the credit. Belong to the first category...there is much less competition.

Indira Gandhi, first woman Prime Minister of India

Outcomes

After reading this chapter you will:
- **Have some ideas about how to deal with your more 'challenging' trustees**
- **Have a better understanding of what motivates them**
- **Be aware of some of the things you might do that make it harder for you**

I have many years of experience in the voluntary sector: as a chief executive, as a trustee, as a chair and as a co-founder of a charity. So I know what it feels like from both sides of the equation. And the single best piece of advice I can give you as a CEO of a charity is to become a trustee. Experiencing what it's like to be a trustee will make you a better chief executive.

Understanding your board

The nature and involvement of trustees in the running of a voluntary organisation is highly dependent upon the size, age and make-up of the organisation concerned. Smaller organisations with fewer staff will often find that their trustees are more involved in the operational side than those that are slightly larger, mainly because in a small charity you often need extra willing and useful hands. The challenge then becomes to ensure that they are able to separate the times when they need to be operating at a strategic level from when they are more involved in the detail.

And this is often where conflict arises: trustees not understanding or respecting the difference between governance and the work of the executive team. My view is that this grey area is flexible and shifting and that there is no absolute right or wrong time or approach. There will be times when trustees either need to be or want to be heavily involved, in times of crisis for example, and other times when they want you just to get on with it. You need to develop the ability to respond appropriately to both situations.

You also need to understand and accept the fact that your 'bosses' are effectively part-time volunteers. This brings special challenges to the relationship. They will not always be available when you need them, for example. They will usually have less of an in-depth understanding about your organisation than you and your staff – and I know that many chief execs and senior staff find this very frustrating. But never forget what a truly effective system of governance this can be. Disregarding personalities for the moment, it is precisely because they are often not involved in the day-to-day running of the organisation that they are more able to avoid getting sidetracked by how things are done, especially if you encourage them to think strategically. Further, and importantly, if you cannot afford to employ the level of experienced staff that your organisation needs, you can compensate for that by ensuring you have specialist, experienced board members who can supply knowledge that you don't have and who give expert advice.

It does amuse me, though, when chief executives complain that their trustees don't engage with the charity enough and, when they do, CEOs then complain that the trustees are interfering!

It's worth remembering that your board members are often deeply committed to the values and cause of the organisation. If you make the effort to work alongside them, to be supportive and understanding, you will have valuable advisers, advocates and supporters.

If your board is not having the kind of discussions or engagement with the organisation that facilitates its development, then you need first to look to yourself and your input to that process. The fact is that a good board is as much about how hard you work at it as it is about the board itself.

Although you are not formally or officially part of the board (which effectively means you don't have voting rights), your role is absolutely critical in keeping members informed and helping them to make the right kinds of decisions and interventions at the right sort of time.

I was working alongside a chief exec who was having real issues with his board. His perception was that they were constantly interfering in the running of the organisation and he was enormously frustrated because he felt that they were challenging his leadership of it. The big issue was one of direction. The board and he disagreed about the right route for the organisation to take. He felt the organisation's best hope for the future was to work more closely with the local authority. His board were absolutely determined to remain independent of what they perceived to be a form of government influence on their work.

He found it deeply irritating that they weren't agreeing with him. There were two things we needed to work on. The first concerned his approach, which wasn't very helpful. He wasn't using the right sort of language or tone in order to get his message across. He came across as very defensive. The second was the real problem: he had forgotten that it is absolutely the right, even the responsibility, of the board to determine the long-term direction of the charity. I think we, as chief execs, forget that at our peril. We are the implementers.

That doesn't mean that we don't have an enormous impact or important role to play on the long-term future of the organisation, but ultimately that is what trustees are there for. In the end, the chief exec left.

Nannies and parents

I think the relationship between the board and the CEO is a bit like the relationships between full-time nannies and working parents. The nanny spends 12 hours a day with the baby and knows what she laughs at; what she will and won't eat; how often her nappy needs changing; when she's cross; when she's tired. They are solely concentrating on the needs of the baby the entire time because that's their job. Then the parents come home and take over and make judgements as to how well the nanny has looked after the baby, because ultimately it is their baby. It must be hard for the parents to walk away and leave the baby with the nanny: they have to trust that the nanny will do what they would do and think is right. And it must be tough for the nanny to know that the baby isn't theirs: they are only taking care of it for the parents. At the end of the day you, as the CEO, are effectively the nanny, qualified in childcare, expert in the baby. That is, qualified to lead the organisation and an expert in what it does. But you are not the one ultimately accountable for the decisions about what is in the long-term best interests of the organisation, just as the nanny is not accountable for the long-term future of the child. Yet you probably feel as committed to the charity as the trustees are – possibly more so. But you need to remember that parents (the trustees) have a right, indeed a duty under law, to be the ultimate arbiter of what is in the long-term best interests of the child (the charity).

With that analogy in mind your job is essentially to advise, inform and deliver. You are the appointed officer of the board. Of course you need to tell them what you think about how the charity is doing and developing, but ultimately you must do as they direct you to do. Having said that, although you are not technically a member of the board, a good chief executive will establish a relationship with trustees so that at board meetings the sense is one of partnership between you and them, so that you all feel you are working together towards the same goal.

However, this will only happen if you have fundamentally agreed on the overall strategy for the organisation. If you don't agree on that you will always be in conflict. Of course you should engage in the organisation's development, put forward your views and ideas and debate when appropriate. But ultimately it's their job to determine the overall strategic direction for the charity and your job to implement it. And if you can't agree on the strategy then I'm afraid it's you who will have to step aside.

But, if you get this right, you and your board will have a dynamic, sometimes frustrating, but ultimately rewarding and successful relationship which enables you and them to lead a powerful and successful organisation.

How boards operate

The make-up and constitution of your board of trustees is dependent upon your governing documents. And contrary to popular opinion, these are not that hard to change. If your board is not working well because its governing documents don't allow it to, then change them.

Ask your board to answer the following questions:

- Do our governance documents reflect the reality of the world we are currently in?
- What do our objects allow and not allow us to do? Do we need to change them in order to move in a new direction?
- Do our governance documents allow us the freedom to develop in new ways in response to future opportunities?
- Do we have the right make-up of board members?
- Do we have the right number of trustees? Should we have more or fewer?
- Do we have the right length of service for trustees?

Having this conversation will help them not only to think about their purpose but also to ensure that your governance is fit for the future.

Getting your board to examine its effectiveness

Is your board effective? Does it know what it needs to do? It can be really difficult to get boards to think about this or get board members properly trained. And that is understandable. Most trustees have other jobs, roles or commitments and are giving up precious time to support you. Getting them to give up even more time to go on courses is a real challenge. But there are ways of getting them to evaluate their own performance without over-complicating things or asking them to give up even more of their time.

I developed a simple questionnaire which you can incorporate into a board meeting or a strategic away day which will help them to ask themselves the right questions and start thinking about how to become an outstanding board.

Feel free to use it and, if these generic questions aren't right for your board, change the questionnaire and put in more appropriate ones.

Boards – good governance

Self-assessment: how well do the following statements describe the performance of the board?

1 The board has a common understanding of the vision/mission/values and strategic objectives

Low | | | | Medium | | | | | High

1	2	3	4	5	6	7	8	9	10

2 The board focuses on strategic issues

Low | | | | Medium | | | | | High

1	2	3	4	5	6	7	8	9	10

3 **The board delegates appropriate authority to the executive team**

Low				Medium					High
1	2	3	4	5	6	7	8	9	10

4 **The board allows the management of the charity to be carried out by the executive team, without undue interference**

Low				Medium					High
1	2	3	4	5	6	7	8	9	10

5 **The board is diverse and representative of the community and people the charity serves**

Low				Medium					High
1	2	3	4	5	6	7	8	9	10

6 **The board regularly reviews its own performance**

Low				Medium					High
1	2	3	4	5	6	7	8	9	10

7 **The board has an open, fair and appropriate recruitment and selection policy for new trustees**

Low				Medium					High
1	2	3	4	5	6	7	8	9	10

8 **The board sets clear terms of reference for sub-committees**

Low				Medium					High
1	2	3	4	5	6	7	8	9	10

9 **The board fully understands its obligations in terms of compliance with its own governing documents and relevant legislation**

Low				Medium					High
1	2	3	4	5	6	7	8	9	10

10 **The board encourages all stakeholders in the charity's planning and decision-making**

Low				Medium					High
1	2	3	4	5	6	7	8	9	10

Why do people become trustees?

From observing and working with a number of trustees in various capacities I have noticed a range of motivations to become a trustee.

There are those who simply feel passionate about the cause of the charity and want to get involved. There are some who know that they have skills, experience and contacts which will be useful to the charity. Then there are those who have fully contributed during their professional lives, often in some completely different field, and feel the need to give back to society in some way. As they are very often senior in background, their preferred route is governance rather than practical work. You rarely find former company directors dishing out the tea or driving the minibus. For some, that is because they realise that their experience may be more useful at board level, but for others it relates to status. Some folk, if they are retired, may well feel an unstated sense of loss of status. This is absolutely not a criticism. It is a completely normal human reaction and one which we simply need to recognise. Some trustees seek to support a charity that has a cause close to their hearts – others don't particularly mind which charity. Some become a trustee because they believe it will enhance their reputation in their community or look good on a CV. Some because they are looking to develop their career in non-executive directorships in all three sectors. And for some, it is because they think the organisation is being run badly and that they will be able to improve things.

The important point to note about the motives is that, actually, they don't matter all that much in terms of the trustees' ability to deliver for the charity. It helps, of course, if you have some understanding of what drives your trustees because that will help you to keep them engaged and motivated. But, critically, what matters most is that the individual is bringing to your board something that enhances the board, such as background, expertise, skill, knowledge, value base or commitment to the cause.

The human side of trustees

It can be very hard when you are working with trustees not to get irritated when they expose their human side: when it appears to you that their egos are getting in the way of you doing your job; when they seem to be more caught up with their relationships with each other or the way the board operates than they are in the work of the charity; when you believe that they are concentrating more on the detailed running of the organisation and not enough on their responsibilities as a board; or when they simply don't get on with each other and you feel like piggy in the middle.

This happens in all charities at some point or another. Even if your board is generally extremely good, the chances are that at some stage things will become difficult. This is because they are people, and have exactly the same issues as everyone else.

I have found that there are some common situations that senior people encounter when dealing with trustees.

- Trustees are elected by each other. This often means that they appoint people who are like themselves and so it can sometimes be hard to get the board to see a different possibility or accept a view that doesn't square with its value set.
- It is common to find a board of trustees with people from very similar backgrounds, education and professional status who bear very little resemblance to the service users or beneficiaries the charity is serving. While it is helpful to have professional expertise, sometimes that brings with it both a lack of understanding about the impact of what they, as the

trustees, do and an undue interference in the day-to-day running of the organisation.

■ Sometimes, the board is so completely different in its make-up that it is hard to stop them fighting and agree on a course of action.

■ Because it is a voluntary role, it can be challenging to get trustees to understand their duties fully and to engage appropriately with the charity.

I developed a checklist of what terrible and brilliant trustees tend to do and a short list of things trustees should know about the executive team to understand them better. Feel free to reproduce these lists and share them with your own trustees.

Ten things that terrible trustees do and brilliant trustees don't

Terry the terrible trustee	*Beryl the brilliant board member*
1. Not making effective use of meetings	
■ Wastes precious board time focusing on the past and not on the future ■ Doesn't remind himself of what happened at the last meeting so time is wasted repeating things ■ Uses electronic devices during the meeting, so people assume he's doing other work ■ Is bad at timekeeping	■ Reads the paperwork well before the meeting to remind herself what happened last time ■ Remembers that trustees only get together for on average 8–12 hours a year so uses that time wisely and strategically ■ During the meeting switches off phones and other electronic devices and focuses on the discussions
2. Forgetting the line between governance and executive functions	
■ Interferes in operational details ■ Forgets about the purpose of the charity ■ Sidesteps the chief executive to direct staff	■ Remembers that getting involved in details blurs the line between governance and executive functions ■ Confines herself to setting or reminding the executive team of the vision and/or direction and allows them freedom to deliver ■ Gets involved in sub-committees or specific projects if needed

3. Not handling crisis well	
■ When faced with a crisis demands more paperwork and/or meetings ■ Assumes someone did something wrong ■ Looks for someone or something to blame ■ Focuses on what happened rather than what can be done	■ Realises that more paperwork doesn't help. If the organisation is sufficiently well structured she recognises that, whether things are going well or badly, different conversations are needed, not more meeting time ■ Doesn't seek to blame anyone or anything ■ Focuses on what's going to happen next
4. Hijacking the meeting	
■ Takes over the meetings or allows fellow trustees to do that ■ Points out spelling or grammar mistakes during the meeting ■ Goes into questioning every detail ■ Raises critical issues at the very end of the meeting	■ Only points out any grammar or spelling mistakes in the paperwork if they are material to decision-making or image and does so in advance of the meeting or afterwards ■ If she has any detailed questions, asks them in advance of the meeting to maximise time during the meeting ■ If she has anything additional to contribute raises it in advance of the meeting so it can go on the agenda or at the very beginning so the chair can decide how to handle it
5. Thinking that the work of trustees is done at the meetings	
■ Doesn't engage with the charity between meetings ■ Fails to respond to emails ■ Has to be chased	■ Engages with the charity between meetings: offers support and expertise when needed ■ Responds to emails promptly ■ Reads communications and responds appropriately (even if to say 'Thanks and well done')

6. Acting as prosecutor, judge, jury and executioner

■ Has a tendency to attack the executive team or assume that something hasn't been done or hasn't been done well ■ Questions aggressively as if he's trying to catch someone out	■ Realises that the board and the executive are a team that needs to work together to achieve the charitable objects and goals of the charity ■ Asks questions that help move things forward

7. Focusing on the wrong things

■ Thinks that the main measure of success is the revenue/ reserves ■ Forgets to keep things in perspective ■ Doesn't focus on the beneficiaries ■ Forgets that it's a board and the majority's decision wins	■ Remembers that revenue is simply one of the resources needed to help achieve the charitable objects ■ Remembers that good times come and go and that it's rarely someone's failure or fault ■ If the board outvotes her, lets it go and moves on

8. Thinking they're the experts

■ Doesn't listen ■ Puts the executive team on the defence ■ Thinks he could do a better job	■ Assumes that the executive team is working hard and doing the right thing so asks questions that are supportive and further the work ■ Recognises that the experts in the charity are the charity staff and dedicated volunteers not the board ■ Treats the executive team as paid professional experts whose job is to advise the board when decisions need to be taken

9. Not acting like a team player	
■ Lets personal interest and opinions get in the way of group decisions ■ Fosters cliques within the board ■ Is obsessed with his own agenda at the expense of group coherence ■ Seeks remuneration for his service ■ Has inappropriate relationships with staff	■ Fosters positive relationships with all other board members and the executive team ■ Helps ensure all trustees have the chance to contribute ■ Appropriately engages with staff ■ Works for the interest of the group, not self-interest ■ Contributes voluntarily
10. Never praising	
■ Tries to catch people doing something wrong	■ Looks for opportunities to praise success and motivate staff

Five useful things every trustee should know about their executive team

1. **They don't care about you.** They care about the beneficiaries (that's how it should be). Their job is to focus on delivering the charitable objectives for the purpose of beneficiaries. And, actually, so is yours. Your job is to make it as easy as possible for them to do theirs.

2. **They won't tell you if you're not a good trustee or a good board.** And that's for obvious reasons, so it is down to you to regularly assess your individual and collective contribution. Always assume you could do better.

3. **Preparing for board meetings takes a huge amount of time.** Every 'quick' paper you ask for because you're interested in something often takes hours of work behind the scenes. And often it's not really that important in the context of delivering against the charity's objects. Be sure that what you're asking for really is strategically and operationally critical. And ask your executive team members if they think that what you're asking for is really needed. Where you can, use existing information or paperwork – don't ask for extra.

4. **They already work long hours and over their contracted time.** Having to attend board meetings out of hours or on a weekend can put even further pressure on them. Try to keep meetings within working hours.

5. **They often hate board meetings.** This is because too often they feel they're being judged negatively or attacked. A good board meeting is when your executive team comes out feeling motivated, supported and with a clear sense of direction.

What's the best way to work with your board?

Your relationship with your board members is primarily down to you. How you engage with them, how you communicate with them, how you respond to them – all affect how well they feel they can work with you.

It's important to note that they will often feel quite powerless. Although it might feel to you that they are all-powerful, really the most they can do is ask you and your team to carry out their wishes. If you don't, the only power they really have is to sack you. And that's not that easy to do. So have some sympathy. They are coming in relatively infrequently, being held to account, asked to make decisions and be supportive about things that they don't have any direct control over.

In my research about the relationships between boards and chief executives there are some common themes about why trustees can find their chief executive difficult. Are you guilty of any of the following?

- Reacting defensively when challenged?
- Responding to suggestions with all the reasons why it can't be done – or saying that you tried it before and it didn't work then?
- Not getting the paperwork to them in plenty of time for them to read and digest?
- Not allowing enough time for discussion at board meetings?
- Reacting to comments/observations made during the meeting without taking time to think and respond appropriately?
- Expecting trustees to fully understand the workings of the organisation?
- Dropping in surprises: announcing things you haven't warned anyone about?
- Not listening to board members' suggestions?
- Explaining at great length why their ideas won't work?
- Not respecting their experience/background/skills/history?
- Not taking them seriously?
- Forgetting that they are the ultimate leaders of the organisation?
- Giving them too much detail...
- ...then complaining that they get involved in the detail?

Also remember that they are, first and foremost, human beings who have needs which are effectively the same as everyone else's. They want to feel they are doing a good job, that they are valued and appreciated, that they are making a difference, that they are cared for and about, that they are more than simply someone doing a job, and that their colleagues (i.e. other members of the board) like and trust them – exactly the same emotions that your staff and other volunteers have about their role in work.

Most of the people who join your board want to do a good job. And there are many trustees who are genuinely very, very good. The problem is how to deal with those trustees who just *feel* difficult to deal with: i.e. you're not quite sure why you find them tricky to handle.

To begin with you need to ask yourself: is the problem here only about your *perception* of them? If you cast your mind back to the leadership styles questionnaire, are you sure that the differences between you are really fundamental, or simply due to the fact that you work in different ways and have forgotten to make allowances?

I think that sometimes, as CEOs, we have very high expectations of our boards which are difficult for them to live up to. We forget that we have lived with the charity every day between board meetings but they haven't. And unless you have communicated with them regularly in between the meetings, they are likely to be concentrating on other things. This means that when they come to the meeting they will probably have completely forgotten the previous conversations (hence why getting the minutes right is so important). So sometimes they seem difficult simply because they're not up-to-date or you haven't communicated with them effectively between meetings.

Your job is as much about managing upward as it is about managing downward. So most of the time if you have a difficult board it's probably within your control. However, there are some difficult buggers out there. Below is a little checklist of truly stereotyped trustees (because it's fun!) and my advice on how to deal with them.

Some examples of difficult behaviours of trustees and how to handle them

Type	Behaviour	How to handle it
The know-it-all	This is the person who believes that they know the best way of dealing with every situation – they often appear to be frustrated during the meetings at what they see as the ignorance of their colleagues and particularly the executive team.	■ Acknowledge their points – don't argue ■ Ask them to clarify precisely what they mean ■ Remind them of progress to date ■ Ask for their ideas and suggestions ■ Ask for examples of what they believe works
The frustrated chief exec	This is the person who thinks they could do a better job of running the charity than the chief exec. They will frequently offer unwanted advice about matters that are not for them to deal with. They will often interfere with minutiae or tell the chief exec/senior team exactly how to carry out a particular task or duty.	■ Ask for their views and opinions ■ Acknowledge their points and say that you will take them into account ■ Don't rise to the bait and get defensive ■ Remind the board often about what is strategic and what is operational by using the appropriate language

The naysayer	This is the person who objects to anything new being proposed.	■ Ask them to explain their objection ■ Ask them if they have an alternative suggestion ■ Ask them to consider the pros and cons of action vs inaction
The critic	This is the person who will look for fault or examples of where things have gone badly or where mistakes have been made – they will seek to apportion blame.	■ Listen and don't react ■ Openly acknowledge mistakes – get in there first! ■ Focus on the future and solutions
The 'duty' attendee	This is the person who turns up at meetings and never contributes much to the discussions – you are never sure what their view is.	■ Ask them directly what they think about a particular point (for example, 'John, I am interested in your view on this') ■ Ask them in advance to contribute to a particular agenda item
The absentee	This is the person who turns up occasionally and rarely engages with the charity in any way other than attending the occasional meeting.	■ Highlight this to your chair and ask them to deal with it ■ Find out what the problem is – do they need some support to attend? ■ Have a register and share it regularly at board meetings ■ Publicly thank and acknowledge those who do attend
The historian	This is the person who has usually been around for a long time and is constantly harping back to the past.	■ Honour the past ■ Acknowledge where the charity has come from and what it has achieved ■ Talk about the need to ensure that the charity is fit for the future ■ Use their historical references to springboard to the current situation/future focus

The volunteer	This is the person who constantly reminds you that they are a volunteer – they will often complain that too much is being asked of them.	■ Grit your teeth! ■ Ask them what they think is reasonable in terms of their time commitment ■ Don't ask them to do more than they are prepared to do
The politician	This is the person who has little interest in the workings of the charity but has a lot to say about its role in the wider context.	■ Dedicate space for this kind of topic on the agenda ■ Remind all trustees regularly that they are *all* accountable for the whole organisation ■ Honour the usefulness of this input – keeps the organisation thinking beyond operational issues

Relationship with the board

Boards differ from the chief exec in one crucial aspect – they are part of a team of peers – so a sense of 'team-ness' will often be very important to them. The truth is, as the CEO you are the only one in any organisational structure who is completely alone. You are not part of the team of the board. You are there to advise and inform. It is right and proper that the board should want some time alone to build up their own relationships. The danger is when this gets out of control and they end up making decisions without involving you.

For many boards, the relationship with the chief executive and senior team can be a very frustrating one. They know, deep in their hearts, that you have more influence on what happens to and in the organisation than they do. They know that they can't *make* you do anything, and that if they force you to do something you don't agree with, you can easily find a way to prove them wrong by ensuring it doesn't work. And even if that is genuinely not what you have done, sometimes it will be perceived that way. Most switched-on boards will realise that the real power base is you and your senior team and that they need to get you onside in order to achieve what they want to achieve.

You need to be very sensitive to this. And don't abuse it. I have seen some chief executives completely ignore the wishes of the board and go their own route, and the board, particularly if it is not a strong one, feels powerless to do anything about it. That isn't good for anyone, least of all the beneficiaries – who are ultimately the ones we are there to serve.

To ensure that the relationship is as positive as it can be there are a number of things you can do.

Firstly, and most importantly, for goodness' sake get the paperwork right! I know it's time-consuming and a pain in the backside – but it's so important. And by paperwork I mean the agenda, the minutes, the board papers and so on.

- Give as much information as you can in the agenda: indicate what type of item it is.
- Make sure all your agenda items are timed.
- Have a summary page of actions in the minutes.

- Make your reports and presentations look professional: that means consistent fonts, layouts and house style.
- DO NOT give too much detail unless it is specifically requested. Keep the information at the right strategic level and you will minimise any tendencies to interfere or to cross the line between executive and board duties.

Below is an example of a helpful agenda. You will note that there is a final page which gives trustees gentle reminders so that they don't get caught out in the meeting and that they have a sense of what preparation, if any, they need to do.

Board meeting sample agenda

Timing	Item	Topic	Leader
17.00–17.10	1	**Minutes and matters arising** **Papers:** ■ Minutes of previous meeting *(For agreement)*	Chair
17.10–17.35	2	**Quarterly leadership report** Trustees have the opportunity to ask questions for clarification on our activities and financial performance in the fourth quarter **Papers:** ■ Quarterly leadership report ■ Operating statement ■ Financial summary ■ Predicted balance sheet ■ Cash flow forecast *(For information)*	CEO + Leadership Team
17.35–18.05	3	**Year end management indicators** *(Presentation for information* *Paper at meeting)*	Ben Wittenberg

18.05–18.25	4	**New brand** *(Presentation)*	Ben Wittenberg
18.25–18.40	5	**Web update** *(Presentation)*	Ben Wittenberg
18.40–18.50	6	**Property update** *(For information)*	Alistair Mortimer/ John Wallace
18.50–18.55	7	**Governance issues** Governance: approval of Auditors' revised Terms of Assignment 2014 Audit fee quotation *(For discussion and agreement)*	John M. de C. Hoare
18.55–19.00	8	**Summary and close** Agreement on future agenda items *(For discussion and agreement)*	Chair

Attendees

Trustees and Officers	Title	Position
Catherine Johnstone	CEO, Samaritans	Chair
Alistair Mortimer	VP, Relationship and Product Management, Bank of America Merrill Lynch	Trustee
Andy Garnett	MD, The Garnett Foundation	Trustee
Caron Bradshaw	CEO, Charity Finance Group	Trustee
Jamie Wilcox	Head of Volunteer Services, Great Ormond Street Hospital	Trustee
Lesley Thornley	CEO, Hull and East Riding CAB	Trustee
John M. de C. Hoare	DSC	Company Secretary

DSC Leadership Team	Title
Debra Allcock Tyler	Chief Executive
Satinder Pujji	Director of Finance
Ben Wittenberg	Director of Development and Delivery
Jay Kennedy	Director of Policy and Research
John Wallace	Director of Operations
Suzanne Tubb	Executive Office
Askar Muhammed	Finance Manager

Notes on Agenda for Trustees

■ Item 3: Year end management indicators

Ben will be giving a presentation which summarises the key highlights of the year in terms of the non-financial indicators. We will give you a hard copy of the data at the meeting for those who want to look at it in more detail.

■ Item 4: DSC brand

Trustees may remember the various papers we have sent you over the last six months, and in particular the one outlining the brand ideas. Having consulted widely, including with you, we have taken on board the various views and have come to a final decision on brand message, logo and colours. Ben will present this to you at the meeting.

■ Item 5: Web update

This is just a short update on how we are progressing with our new DSC website.

■ Item 6: Property update

Alistair has already largely kept you up to date via email on property so this item is mainly an opportunity for questions.

■ Item 7: Governance issues

This short item, led by John Hoare, is a standard item at this time of year as we go into our audit period.

Minutes

When it comes to the minutes clearly they need to be fairly full as they are a legal record of what was discussed at the meeting and may be needed for reference if anything goes wrong or decisions get challenged. But for practical purposes in terms of running the charity the key thing is to identify actions and make sure that they are reported. At DSC we extract the key actions from the minutes and put them onto a separate document so that they are clear. We also make sure that before they are sent out with the board papers we have indicated how we've progressed against the actions (by including an additional column called 'Update' specifically for that). This saves lots of time at the actual board meeting.

Example action summary from minutes
Action points

Page		Action by whom:	Action by when:	Update
1.	**Headshots for DSC website** Headshots of Andy Garnett and Lesley Thornley for DSC website still outstanding. To be taken prior to next meeting.	Senior Team	27-Jan-16	Headshots will be taken before meeting
7.	**Collaboration** Trustees discussed the pros and cons of collaborative work and decided that this would be a strategic conversation for a later date. **Potential partner** AG informed the meeting that he is off to meet a potential partner and feels that there is a fantastic amount of opportunity here for DSC which he will research and report back to this meeting at a later date.	Chair and Trustees Andy Garnett	Agenda item during 2016 27-Jan-16	Discuss with Trustees Awaiting update from AG
8.	**Chair of Acevo** Catherine and Debra have arranged to meet with Paul Farmer, Chair of Acevo, on Tuesday 1 March 2016	Suzanne	Dates being sent to PF office	Completed

Page		Action by whom:	Action by when:	Update
12.	**DSC's achievements/ DSC's positioning** Chair suggested that a bigger conversation about (1) what DSC's achievements might be, (2) what is going on in the sector and (3) DSC's positioning, should take place. Form a working group/ Trustees sub-committee involving DSC Trustees and DSC staff interested in policy. DSC Executive Team to take this idea away and set something up for 2016.	Executive Team	May-16	For discussion at 5-BOT/LT meeting
13.	**Resend DSC 2016 board dates** Resend 2016 Board of Trustees meeting dates to all Trustees.	Suzanne	27-Jan-16	Completed

If you want your relationship with the board to be as successful as possible, try to make it easier for trustees to do their job – you will see that this benefits you as much as it helps them:

1. Have a conversation to clarify what their expectations are of you and your senior team and what your expectations are of them.
2. Agree what is reasonable in terms of preparation for board meetings (i.e. what requires paperwork in advance and what doesn't, and what to do if an issue crops up on which you don't have time to prepare a paper).
3. Ensure that you have an agenda, agreed in advance with your chair, which specifies each agenda item, the nature of the discussion and how long each item will take.
4. Minute your meetings against agenda items so that trustees find it easier to keep track.
5. Keep them updated on progress regularly – even outside normal board meetings.

6. Try to avoid surprising them – particularly with bad news! (Having said that, sometimes you will be accused of surprising them when actually you didn't know either. This is the point at which you simply grit your teeth and acknowledge their worry.)

One final, and I think extremely important, tip. You should have one-on-one time with every member of your board at least once a year. This enables you to build up a relationship with them, allows them to share their thinking directly with you and gives you an opportunity to explain your thinking to them. It takes time but is worth doing. I've done it every year that I've been a CEO, apart from one year when I had too much on my plate so I allowed my meetings with them to slip. Without going into gory details, I very nearly lost my job at the end of that year and I'm pretty sure that if I'd paid better attention to the needs of my board the difficult situation we ended up in would have been at the very least mitigated, if not avoided altogether. The trustees matter. Pay attention to them.

What should you ask of your trustees?
- To turn up to meetings on time and to stay to the end.
- To read the paperwork in advance of the meeting and to make notes in advance of their questions.
- To tell you in advance if there is a problem/issue they want to raise at the meeting so that you can prepare for it.
- To discuss openly and honestly with you any issues they may have with your leadership of the organisation.
- To involve you in all their decision-making.
- To chastise you in private and support you in public.
- To remember that *you* can never take credit for good performance because as an effective leader your job is to apportion credit and absorb blame – but that success in any area does have a lot to do with your leadership.

What you should expect
- They will not remember things between meetings – usually they have other work/jobs/interests which is the primary focus for them and it is not reasonable for you to expect that they will always remember what you have told them before.
- They will not always act as one – they will frequently disagree with one another – and this is not necessarily an example of board disunity. Disagreement is healthy if handled well.
- They will not think that you are the best thing since sliced bread – they are very aware that your performance reflects on them and so they are more likely to be critical than not. That's fair enough and you need to learn not to take it personally.

- They will not always agree that you know what is best for the organisation; indeed, they will believe that they are the ones who should know, and so they should.
- Not all of them will trust or respect you – you need only to make sure that the majority do, and concentrate on them. Don't waste time trying to win over a trustee who isn't 'winoverable'! Let your chair deal with them.

Your relationship with your chair

Firstly, it's important for you both to remember that technically (unless it's specified in your memorandum and articles of association) you don't actually report to the chair. Ultimately you report to the *whole* board and they are all accountable for your performance. The chair effectively acts as a stand-in for the board, for practical and pragmatic reasons. So it's important that you don't let your relationship with your chair become so close that you effectively exclude the rest of the board, otherwise you will both find it difficult to carry out your respective roles.

There is also always the danger that the other trustees will see you and your chair as being in cahoots and, therefore, an atmosphere of distrust may build up.

It is undoubtedly true that you need to build up a strong relationship with your chair, one that is mutually open and honest. This is not always easy. Many of the most stressed and anxious chief execs I know are that way because they don't feel they're supported by their chair. However, it's a two-way street. You chair also needs to feel supported by you.

And you both need to understand and agree your roles. I tend to feel that the relationship is at its most effective when the chair sees their role as to manage the board and represent the executive team to the trustees, and the chief exec sees their role as to manage the charity team and represent the board to the staff.

Here are some tips for building a strong relationship with your chair:

- Meet regularly face-to-face. Probably monthly as a minimum, more if you need to.
- Keep them updated between meetings: short notes just to let them know how things are progressing.
- Keep them in the loop about any interactions you have with other board members. Don't let them be caught on the hop!
- Don't give them any surprises. 'If in doubt, shout it out!' should be your motto here. Your chair is there to support you and if you don't keep them informed they won't be able to lead the board effectively.
- Work with them on board paperwork. Agree agenda items during one-to-ones. Share tactics about how to get the work done.

Some critical dos and don'ts!

DO
- Remember your board is made up of human beings too
- Encourage your board to recruit openly for trustees
- Make use of their skill and expertise
- Take control by adjusting the way you react to your board
- Help them to concentrate on strategic issues by using the appropriate language

DON'T
- Forget they are only part-time and volunteers
- Allow them to accept as a new trustee someone who already has too many other trusteeships
- Forget to listen to their advice
- Get cross when they get it wrong
- Give them too much detailed operational information if it's not appropriate

7 Survival isn't mandatory

You don't have to change. Survival isn't mandatory. Attributed to Dr W. Edwards Deming, American statistician

Outcomes

After reading this chapter you will:
- Be clear about why organisations need to change
- Be sensitive to why people resist change
- Have some ideas about how to implement change

This chapter is about why organisations need to constantly change, how to engage your organisation in change and why one of your most fundamental jobs as a leader at the top of the organisation is to create change, even if the organisation apparently doesn't need to.

Why change?

Actually, this isn't as daft a question as it sounds. Your organisation is doing a good job. You have tried and tested methods of achieving your objectives which are still working. You are managing to attract the sort of funding that you need in order to continue with your work. And you've been around a long time. So why on earth would you change?

Well, the problem is that the world around us is always changing, whether we like it or not. And even if fundamental problems don't necessarily change (there are still the poor, the sick, the socially disadvantaged, natural disasters, etc.), the way in which those problems manifest themselves and the expectations of the people affected by those problems change. If we are not constantly looking to see what our external environment is like and what we need to do to adapt to it, then eventually we will find that what works now no longer works and that we haven't got the ability, resources or time to change enough to keep up.

Often, because we are doing well at something, we forget to think about what else might be possible. Our thinking becomes limited to what we know, or assume we know. To illustrate this point, try this task.

Join up the following nine dots in four straight lines *without* taking your pen off the paper.

Some of you will know how to do this because you have seen it before. But many of you will not realise how it's done and be unable to do it. To see how to do it, turn to the end of the chapter.

The reason that many of you can't do it immediately is because you see the shape of the nine dots as the shape of a box. You assume, even though you were not told this, that you have to stay within the shape of the box. And the problem is not solvable unless you draw your lines outside the apparent box shape.

So often we see our organisations in that box shape. 'Box' language includes things like:

'We've always done it this way.'

'It's worked for years.'

'This is what our organisation stands for.'

'This is the best way.'

'There is no other way.'

'We tried it before and it didn't work then.'

'The trustees/volunteers/staff/beneficiaries/funders won't like it.'

'Box' language creates 'box' thinking. We are unable to think of new and different ways of doing things because we are making certain assumptions about how our world will be in the future.

The sigmoid curve

Some of you may be familiar with the sigmoid curve. This curve is a mathematical expression which describes a rate of growth which is rapid and then declines. This produces a curve that appears as an S, due to this slow start. There is then a period of rapid growth, followed by a levelling out and eventually potentially declining. Many biological and ecological systems follow this structure (for instance, population growth) and its pattern has been replicated in studies of product life cycles and societal trends.

The eminent writer Charles Handy believes that the sigmoid curve also applies to the growth and development of organisations. He argues that the best time to create the new curve for your organisation is before it peaks. In some ways this is harder to do, because it is difficult to recognise

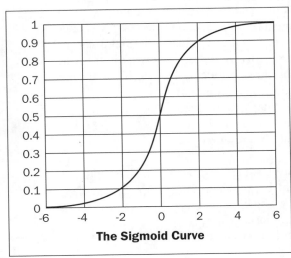

The Sigmoid Curve

the need for change (or indeed, to get others to) during a period of success. Nonetheless it is vital. Most organisations don't see the need for change until the curve is on its downward trend, which means that you begin the change process during a period of 'failure' when resources are likely to be more limited, people are likely to be demoralised and the focus will be on what's going wrong or what went wrong rather than the more important question of what's possible for the future.

So the point at which to look at creating change is when the organisation appears to be on the upper part of the trend, before it starts to level out. In fact,

the most successful organisations are constantly looking to see what needs to change.

This is the point at which you will often hear people use those worn out phrases such as 'if it ain't broke don't fix it', 'don't tamper with success' and so on. The point is that it doesn't have to be broken to be useless in the future. Take video cassette recorders for example. They weren't broken, they worked perfectly well, but the pace of change means that you can't buy them any more. We went from VCRs to DVDs and MP3 players, and now modern technology is such that we don't even need a recording machine to record programmes or films from the TV. In fact, you don't

—— **change strategy**
- - - - - **no change strategy**

need a separate television if you have a computer. We don't need floppy disks, CDs or USB memory keys any more because we now have the cloud. And so on.

If we don't keep up, we will be left out. It really is that simple.

Your job as a leader is to be always looking to the future – imagining what might be different, what the new issues might be, how what is happening in the broader context may affect what happens to your organisation and its ability to carry out its work in the longer term. You don't even need to have the answers. What you need to do is make sure that the questions are being asked.

Why are people resistant to change?

Many of us will have experienced people being resistant to change. And it is important to understand why that is. They are afraid that they might lose their jobs or their status in the organisation, or that they will end up with more work or responsibilities they don't feel ready for. And these are completely valid fears because, truthfully, change, especially big change, often involves redundancies or changes in job descriptions.

Further, change is often not handled particularly well. People are not involved in identifying the need for change so, by the time they hear about it, the wheels are already in motion and people are thrust into the change process about halfway through. And because they were not involved at the identification stage they tend to see proposals for change as criticism of what has gone on in the past or the quality of their current work.

It is likely, then, that you will meet an element of this thinking when you are proposing change. It is important that you, as the change initiator, recognise that decisions taken in the past were valid decisions based on the needs of that particular moment. If you want to derail your change quickly then blame the need to change on failures in the past!

People are often also afraid because they fear that change is irrevocable and that they will be stuck with something they hate and that doesn't work.

I have observed that when change is implemented there are a series of stages that people often go through in reaction to the change, which remind me of what happens during a normal grieving process.

Stage 1 Shock/surprise
Stage 2 Denial
Stage 3 Cognitive acceptance
Stage 4 Emotional acceptance
Stage 5 Engagement

Stage	Typical reactions
1 Shock/surprise	■ Perception that someone is to blame ■ Doubts in their own competence or the competence of others ■ Distrust of leaders proposing the change
2 Denial	■ Questioning the need to change ■ Arguing for the status quo ■ Pointing out the negative consequences of change ■ Grumbling and being upset
3 Cognitive acceptance	■ Understanding of the rationale ■ Asking questions about process and impact ■ Arguing for alternatives
4 Emotional acceptance	■ Feeling the need for change ■ Expressing few grumbles ■ Possibly generating excitement and optimism
5 Engagement	■ Becoming involved in solutions ■ Coming up with ideas ■ Being willing to experiment ■ Showing willingness to learn new things

I don't think you can shortcut any of these stages. But if you are sensitive to what people go through, you can minimise the damage caused at the early stages and move people faster through the process towards engagement.

Do not underestimate the emotional impact that change has on people. And don't ignore it. If you ignore the emotional response, or dismiss it as irrelevant, you will seriously hamper your ability to see the change process through.

> GRRR...YOU COME IN HERE AND START CHANGING EVERYTHING

Nowadays organisations cannot guarantee employment; indeed, voluntary organisations and charities never have been able to. In place of this, however, we can guarantee employability. In other words, we can equip our people with the ability to respond openly and willingly to change and give them the emotional skills to feel positive and excited about change, wherever they are working.

So, people are more likely to engage if you can help them to realise that the more they get used to change the better equipped they are not just for the organisation's future but also for their own future.

How to get the organisation to change

The approach that you take to initiating change is quite important. Focus on the future and what the organisation needs to look like in order to achieve the objective.

Importantly, honour the past. Help people to understand that the need for change is not necessarily due to the organisation failing to do things properly in the past, or due to previous poor management, or due to staff/volunteers not doing a good job. The change is in response to circumstances existing today and those that are likely to exist tomorrow.

My favourite change phrase is 'Honour the past – don't live in it'. Kriss Akabusi, the gold-medal-winning athlete says, 'The past is for reference and not for residence'. I think this is a useful way of thinking and talking about why we shouldn't cling to the past. Someone once said that the difference between the voluntary sector and the private sector is that private sector organisations are usually looking ahead to where they're going and voluntary sector organisations are very often looking behind themselves at where they came from. That's all well and good, but while you're looking behind yourself and feeling proud of the past, you don't see the hole in the road that you're about to fall into.

To engage people in change of course acknowledge history, but get them to think about how to make that 'history' last a bit longer!

To do this, involve people at the very beginning of the change process. That is *at the stage at which you think change might be necessary but you don't know what or why or how*! There are a number of techniques for doing this.

The PESTLE model

One of the ways to get people engaged in thinking about the need for change without feeling criticised is to use the PESTLE model.

Political
Environmental (I usually interpret this to mean our 'market place')
Societal
Technological
Legal
Economic

It is a way of looking at the things that affect your organisation and asking yourself what impact they will have and what you can do about it.

So you ask questions at your trustee meetings or your senior management team meetings such as:

- What is happening in the political arena at the moment? For instance, what are the local authority's priorities for the next few years? Has there been a change in council leadership? What does that mean and what could we do about it?
- What is happening in our environment/market at the moment? What are the trends? Are there other charities doing the same as us? Are we the best at what we do? How could we be better?

And so on.

You should also be asking these questions of your management team, indeed of all the staff in your organisation. And certainly at the staff level you should be asking questions such as:

- What are we doing well?
- What are we doing less well?
- What are we not doing that we should be doing?
- What are we doing that we shouldn't be doing?
- What could we do differently/better for the future?

It has been my experience that if you ask staff what could be done differently they nearly always know! And if you ask them in the context of improving what you do and the way in which you do it, usually they will have lots of suggestions to make. And if you have asked them they are much more likely to participate, if not enthusiastically, then at least not reluctantly, in the change process.

However, in bringing about successful change remember to think about the following questions:

1. Be clear about the vision behind the change: what is this change going to achieve for the organisation?
2. What is the change motivator? That is, what is it that is happening or is going to happen that makes the change matter?
3. What is the capacity for the change? In other words, how open are people to it? What will you need to do to engage them in the process? Do you have the resources to cope?
4. Consider first steps: what are the things that you can do to begin the change process that will feel like immediate steps and will be successful?

To deal with people's fears it is important to reassure them that if the change doesn't work then you won't stick with it. A good approach is to talk about the need to experiment: 'let's try things out and see if we can make it work'. This approach reduces the fear that people will be stuck with something unworkable. There may be some who will see it as an opportunity to *prove* to you that the change won't work. But the vast majority, your critical mass (see Chapter 1), will feel more empowered to see if they can make it work.

The Moses metaphor

I came across a great metaphor for change from two American writers, William Bridges and Susan Mitchell. This is a useful way to think about what happens during the change process.

However, do bear in mind that, when thinking about change in the context of this metaphor, change is actually continuous. The common mistake that people make is thinking that if they change something, that'll be it. Actually change is ongoing which is why it is so important to ensure that your people understand that you don't arrive, breathe a sigh of relief and celebrate that the change is over. It is constant.

If you know the story of Moses the key elements, in this context, are that he realised change had to happen, created the vision of a land of milk and honey and convinced the Pharaoh to let him lead his people out of Egypt. He then parted the waters of the Red Sea and they closed behind him, spent 40 years wandering around in the wilderness, found Mount Sinai and got the Ten Commandments, and handed over leadership to Joshua who eventually led the people to the Promised Land.

As a metaphor for change there are a number of elements to consider.

The story: a vision of a land of milk and honey

What's really going on?

Moses is painting a picture of a possible new future to inspire people.

What can you do?

- Identify the 'land of milk and honey' for your organisation – how is it going to be better and why?
- Express it simply and clearly in a way that inspires people.
- Use language that helps your managers to continually emphasise the reason for the change in a positive way.

The story: convincing the Pharaoh to let go

What's really going on?

In bringing down plagues Moses was essentially highlighting the consequences of not changing.

What can you do?

- Consider and think about the 'inner pharaohs': those internal fears and thoughts that prevent us from taking action.
- Anticipate people's resistance and think of ways to overcome it.
- Highlight the problems – don't rush to solve them independently of the change process – they add impetus to your change process.

The story: parting the Red Sea

What's really going on?

This was a big win for Moses – it was an immediate first success on the journey which reinforced the action.

What can you do?

- Make sure you build in some early quick wins to show people that it's the right decision.
- Communicate them across the organisation.

The story: closing the Red Sea

What's really going on?

When the waters closed behind them there was no going back.

What can you do?

- Change something that can't be changed back.
- Encourage people to focus on the new direction.

The story: wandering about in the wilderness

What's really going on?

This was the stage at which the first push was over and they had to settle into the long journey. People got tired, dispirited and hungry, convinced they'd passed that precise bush and camel several weeks ago and not sure if the choice was the right one. They needed sustenance and hope.

What can you do?

- Recognise that in any change process there is a transition period when it isn't clear what's happening or how things are going or when it appears to be slow and plodding.
- Don't be tempted to rush things because people are impatient or demoralised.
- Provide 'sustenance' for your people in the form of lots and lots of information, updates on progress, consultation forums and feedback mechanisms: point out successes and acknowledge mistakes and failures.
- Keep communicating the 'land of milk and honey' message but remind people that this is a continuing process.

The story: Mount Sinai and the Ten Commandments

What's really going on?
The 'new rules' for the 'new world'.

What can you do?

- As soon as you can capture new ways of working or processes get them written up and communicated, both in writing and orally.
- Celebrate successes.

The story: handing over to Joshua

What's really going on?
Recognising that a different kind of leadership is needed for the next stage.

What can you do?

- Let go.
- Trust others to continue the change process for you.
- Empower your managers to take more decisions and continue to think of new possibilities.
- Re-emphasise the need to keep looking for change.

The story: arriving at the Promised Land

What's really going on?
They get there.

What can you do?

- You won't! Precisely because change is ongoing.
- Look at your environment – has your Promised Land become Egypt?
- What's changed or is going to change in the external world that means you need to change again?
- What new things do you need to do?
- Keep your communications mechanisms going – feedback, consultations, improvement groups and so on.
- Keep people conscious of the constant need to change.

Did it work?

Do you know what? Probably not. What I mean is that a plan is only good until you put it into action, when suddenly all sorts of things pop out of the woodwork that you hadn't anticipated. It is highly unlikely that you will have identified what needs to change, how you want it to change and by when – and then find it happens exactly as planned. This is the real world. It doesn't.

So what do you need to do? Well, have some measures of success in mind which are about the outcome, *not* the process. What do you want to be different? Is it? Don't focus necessarily on how you want it to be different. For example, if you want to improve your service to your user group, has it been improved? Who judges it? It may be that the very process of implementing your plans brought about new plans and ideas and you still effectively reached your end goal.

And, above all, keep communicating with people about what's working, what isn't and what's happening next.

Managing change is like piloting a sailing ship. You almost never get to your final destination via the route you planned. The wind turns in the wrong direction and you have to tack (change your course) or the weather gets up and you have to stop in port a little longer than you had planned, and so on. The trick is to be responsive to what might happen, realise that you probably won't anticipate most of what might happen (who can read into the future?) and make sure your ship is light and flexible enough to respond appropriately.

Change is not simply about what actions you do or don't take. It's about what you achieve at the end.

Some critical dos and don'ts!

DO	DON'T
■ Involve people at the very beginning of the change process	■ Think you don't need to change
■ Initiate change by encouraging people to think about the external environment	■ Blame the need for change on things that were wrong in the past
■ Keep people informed all the way through the change process	■ Forget to link change to the achievement of your overall vision
■ Seek to change even if things are going well	■ Ignore people's emotional responses to change

Solution to the nine dots problem

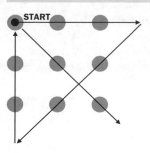

8 Networks and big set pieces

You just stay here in this one corner of the Forest waiting for the others to come to you. Why don't you go to them sometimes?
A. A. Milne, Rabbit addresses Eeyore in *The House at Pooh Corner*

Outcomes

After reading this chapter you will:
- **Know how to network effectively**
- **Have some tips and ideas about how to give really powerful presentations**

As someone at the top of the organisation it is highly likely that you are going to have to communicate in public – that is, with people outside your organisation – either formally through presentations or informally through networking. This chapter looks at how to make sure that you are credible in these environments.

Networking

> If you approach each new person you meet in a spirit of adventure, you will find you become increasingly interested in them and endlessly fascinated by the new channels of thought and experience and personality that you encounter.
>
> Eleanor Roosevelt, *You Learn by Living*

Networking is one of the things I, and many of the chief execs and senior people that I speak to, find the hardest thing to do – particularly when we are alone among strangers. But actually, it's not that hard to do if you don't think of it as a chore to be done, but rather as a way of getting to know people who you might like.

There was a senior figure in the voluntary and community sector who had the reputation of being a consummate networker because he was known to a lot of people and he made a really concerted effort to do it. However, the problem was that when he was talking to you at a function you could tell he wasn't really listening. His eyes were constantly looking over your shoulder and you felt he was looking for someone more interesting or more important to talk to. That may not have been the case, but it certainly felt like it.

People will know if you are a chore on their list or if you are only talking to them because you want something from them. And for me, networking is about creating an opportunity to build a meaningful and useful relationship – not just to have people recognise your name.

I don't think of it as networking. I think of it as making new friends, not necessarily for me personally (although that can be a rather lovely consequence of powerful networking) but for my organisation.

The classic networking mistake is to spend your time talking about your organisation. If you want people to listen to you, you have to first begin by listening to them. What's going on in their world? What are their problems? What are they interested in? You know, I've made an awful lot of professional friends by simply asking them if they were happy! I asked that question because actually I'm always curious about whether people are or not, so it's genuine. But it comes as such a surprise to people that, very often, they completely open up and you get the chance to forge something real rather than something expedient. However, this is just my preference. If you network for expedience only, that's probably fine. But just don't expect it to be lasting.

Also, if you're networking for relationships, then you will probably find that you don't get much in the short term. But that investment will pay off later. Oh, and don't forget – people do know if you're faking it!

The following checklist of networking is inspired by *Empower Yourself: Self development for women* by Eve Warren and Caroline Gielnik.

What to do	External networking
Be clear about what you want	Know what outcome you would like as a result of this networking – it may only be to have people know who you are.
Approach people first	This is the really hard bit and the bit I personally hate the most. However, most of us feel uncomfortable in situations where we don't know anyone, even those who seem particularly confident. Simply start by introducing yourself and then ask about them. Who are they? Why are they at this particular event? What does their organisation do? How is it doing? Look for common ground.
Give a firm handshake	This sounds a bit obvious but you'd be amazed how many people have a limp handshake or don't bother at all.

Introduce positively	Speak positively about who you are and what you do. Don't assume that people will know who you are or what your organisation does. And if they don't they may feel they ought to and be too uncomfortable to ask. Tell them about the work of your organisation.
Make the conversation two-way	Let them do most of the talking, but make sure that you also share a little about yourself. If they have been really open and honest, reflect that by being the same yourself.
Find a way to remember them	This is a big problem for me! I meet a lot of people and can recognise faces but rarely names. Collect business cards. Notice something specific about them that might help you to recall them at a later date (for example, something they once did or something you have in common).
Circulate	But not too obviously. Don't spend all your time at events hanging out with the people you already know. Try to spend time with people you don't. And one of the easiest ways to do that is to invite people to join in the group that you are talking with. There is always someone on their own looking awkward. Invite them to join your group – even if you yourself are with strangers.
Maintain contact after the event	This is the bit that really matters. Networking, for me, is about building relationships. That happens after the event. Send a quick email to say 'nice to meet you!' and possibly suggest meeting for a drink or lunch.

Be generous in your networking. I share my friends around. If I think there are two people who would get on well or ought to meet each other I try to make sure it happens.

SORRY! CAN'T STOP —
YOU'RE NOT ON MY LIST...

CONFERENCE

MEET & GREET

Big set pieces

One of the results of your successful networking might well be that you are called upon to give a speech or formal presentation. You are likely to have to do this anyhow at some point during your leadership. The larger your organisation, the more this will be necessary, although whatever the size of your organisation, you do need to ensure that you are competent in this kind of delivery. Interestingly, big set pieces are the ones that tend to make people the most nervous and for which they spend the most time preparing, yet, actually, they are the least critical in terms of your impact on your organisation's ability to deliver. Nonetheless, they are still important.

Depending on which surveys you look at, fear of public speaking is the number one fear, or second only to spiders (and above the fear of death), or at least in the top ten or so of things that people most fear. I've heard it said about public speaking that the human brain is a remarkable thing – it works from the moment you're born until the moment you stand up to speak in public!

The following advice applies whether you are delivering a set piece to your own organisation's staff or volunteers or to a group of people you don't know. Making an effective public presentation begins long before you actually stand on the platform and deliver. You need to know who your audience is and what the venue is like by answering the following questions.

Audience

- Who is your audience? What are their roles?
- If you are seeking funding or support, then who is the decision-maker? How do they make decisions?
- What are they interested in? And don't guess! In my early days in the voluntary sector I was asked to give a speech to about 20 chief executives of reasonably sized charities. I made an assumption that they wanted to know about the detailed make-up of the voluntary sector. So that's the speech I prepared and delivered. What they actually wanted to know about was the difference in leadership behaviours between the voluntary sector and the private sector. My speech went down like a lead balloon! One phone call to the organiser would have made sure I was talking about the right thing.
- What do they already know? (In my example above, they knew more about the sector than I did!)
- What are their expectations?

- What will they have already heard? Who has spoken before you? What were they talking about? How did the audience react?
- How are they likely to listen? Are they likely to be a fairly cynical audience? Will they hang on your every word?
- In what context will they be listening? What is their state of mind? Is it the end of a long day? Have they heard loads of presentations about the same subject already?

Venue

- How is the room laid out? Where will you be in relation to your audience?
- Are you expected to stand on a platform or behind a lectern? Don't be bullied by the organisers here – if you don't like lecterns don't use them. Or if you prefer a lectern, ask for one. What will the lighting levels be like? Again, here you do not have to be spotlighted on a stage if you don't want to be. Personally, I hate it and always ask the organisers to turn on the house lights. I prefer to see who I am talking to and gauge their reactions as I am speaking. And I would *strongly* advise against using PowerPoint for anything other than visuals, including graphs or photographs – but more on that later.

Focus on the outcome

You need to be really clear about what you want to achieve as a result of your presentation, as that will make a big difference to the content you include and how you deliver it.

Many people confuse the purpose of a presentation with the outcome. You should focus on what change you want to see in the audience as a result of your presentation, i.e. the outcome.

Generally speaking there are six reasons for presenting:

1. To brief (update or inform)

In other words, you want to impart some information. But actually the real objective is not about imparting the information, but about the audience understanding and remembering what it is you have told them. Therefore...

Outcome: to have the audience understand and retain a piece of information.

How?

- Use simple language that they will understand.
- Keep to no more than three key points – they won't remember more.
- Use real examples that they can identify with.

2. To instruct (inform or teach)

Here you want your audience to learn something – but that is specifically because you want them to do something with what they have learned. Therefore...

Outcome: to have the audience understand, remember and act on their learning.

How?

- Build in some way of them practising what they have learned.
- Build in time for them to think about or share what action they will take.

3. To inspire (inspire or motivate)

Here you want your audience to be inspired by what you have said – often, again, to bring about some kind of action. Therefore…

Outcome: to make the audience feel excited and enthused.

How?

- Use powerful, simple language.
- Tell stories.
- Avoid statistics and data.
- Use visuals.

4. To advocate (convince or sell a point of view)

Here you want your audience to be your ambassadors after your presentation, or to give you the funds or the project or the contract. Therefore…

Outcome: to get the audience to believe in your case as if it were their own – or to buy/donate/sponsor/support.

How?

- Use examples from their experience.
- Get them to imagine what it would be like if it was them in this situation/plight.
- Use real examples and stories.
- Show them what's in it for them.
- Appeal to people's emotions.

5. To stimulate (discussion and debate)

Here you are aiming to get your audience actively engaged and drawing their own conclusions. Therefore…

Outcome: to get the audience to talk and think about the issue.

How?

- Make plenty of time during your presentation for them to talk to one another.
- Pose questions – real ones that they have to think about to answer.

6. To gratify (entertain or amuse)

Here you are aiming for the feel-good factor. Therefore…

Objective: to send them away laughing and feeling good.

How?

- If you are not a natural joke teller then don't tell jokes – tell funny stories, based on true events.
- Exaggerate to enhance the humorous aspects.
- Take the mickey out of yourself and your own experiences.

Being clear about the outcome will help you to make your presentation more powerful. For example, if you want to stimulate discussion and debate, then get your audience to speak to each other during your presentation. Build in time for them to discuss what you have said.

If you want your audience to feel inspired you might build in some kind of physical activity to get their adrenaline going, or show them a graphic photograph, or use poetry or quotations.

Always think in terms of outcomes not objectives. Objectives might indicate some of what you need to include in your content – but thinking of outcomes is more likely to produce the kinds of results you're interested in.

Structure

Structuring your presentation is, in fact, one of the easier aspects.

Opening

Make it punchy and memorable. Even if what you are talking about doesn't seem exciting on paper, you can make it sound exciting by how you draw attention to it in the opening part of your presentation. The following topic is not exactly inspirational, but if you compare the two openers you can see how the speaker made it seem as if it mattered.

Snooze in five seconds...

During the previous fiscal year the French voluntary sector had access to in excess of 25% of an EU-funded grant, voted for and agreed on by the key voice agencies in the regional development arena, with no particular bias or prejudice evident at any of the application stages. In comparing giving data for the year, it is clear that the British voluntary sector did not fare so well. Intensive investigations have led us to the conclusion that, while there are many factors which influence the awarding of the grant, the primary factor is the failure of the British voluntary sector to both understand and work within the clearly laid out guidelines and procedures necessary to ensure successful applications. This is a situation that we need to rectify.

Got me awake!

Last year the French received 25% of the European Regional Development Grant. Guess what the Brits got? 3%! Why? Because we don't know how to use the system. This presentation is going to show you how.

You want your audience to know immediately that what you are going to say is interesting – so don't use long words and clever jargon. Keep it punchy and try to include something that will immediately make them sit up and pay attention. And get that point in in the first few sentences.

Middle

Don't put in more than three to five key points. Any more than that and people won't remember. The fact is that most of us cram far too much information into our presentations. Why do people say too much? They may be keen to demonstrate what they know, they want to be helpful, they want to demonstrate they have done their homework or perhaps they simply love their subject and could bang on about it for hours. You need to limit the information.

If you think about it, if during a presentation someone gave you 100 facts, how many would you remember? What about ten facts? Well you might remember 5% of 100 facts (and you have no way of ensuring that the five facts they remember are the most important ones!). Your audience might remember 50% of ten facts (but again, are they the ones you want them to remember?). So if people are only going to remember around five facts why not only give them five facts? – the ones that you actually want them to remember because you believe they are the most important.

The point is that people don't remember much of what they simply hear. So you do need to concentrate on a small number of key points. No more than five – and probably the optimum is three.

If you think about the pieces of information that had most impact on their audiences compare the following:

The Sermon on the Mount **100 words**
The American Declaration of Independence **500 words**
The EU Directive on aubergines **7,000 words**

I rest my case!

In the main content of your presentation *use examples*, and try to avoid making them hypothetical. Real examples, either yours or others', are much more powerful at getting your message across. *Stories not stats* is the rule of thumb here.

End

Make it clear that you have ended – and have a concluding sentence which is punchy and adds to the content. Always end the presentation with something like 'Thank you for listening'. That honours the audience and makes it clear that you have finished. Again, avoid long drawn-out paragraphs with loads of detail and – that classic of all presenter mistakes – the never-ending ending: '...and finally...oooh, and also finally...and finally, finally.'

For example: 'The British voluntary sector can achieve 50% of the EU Regional Development Grant. Thirteen billion euros! Just follow my advice. Thank you for listening.'

And finally and most importantly, as someone once said, the best way to make people think you know what you're talking about – is to know what you're talking about!

Winning your audience

If you think about the best speakers you have heard, you will probably find that they share some of the following things in common. All you need to do is practise the same things. They:

- vary their pace (volume and tone differ at different points);
- speak directly to the audience;
- have plenty of eye contact;
- come across as friendly and approachable;
- seem to be natural – themselves;
- pause often;
- think before answering a question;
- smile frequently;
- use colloquialisms;
- use informal language;
- keep the number of points they make to the minimum;
- use visual imagery;
- allow the audience to use their imagination: they don't provide all the pictures for them;
- tell a story;
- avoid abstract language (you know those speakers who use big, clever language when simple words would be much easier to understand and much easier to remember).

When you are giving an oral presentation it is really important that you don't confuse language that is meant for the eye with language that is meant for the ear. Spoken language needs to concentrate on words that immediately bring visual imagery to the audience's minds. For example, what would you immediately think of if I used the term 'wealth-creation unit'? How about 'livestock asset'? Alright, what about 'bovine resource'? Well, would it be easier if I just used the term 'cow'? Get the point?

Keep your language simple and easily imaginable!

Visual aids

I want to end by talking about the use of visual aids. Why do we use visual aids? Well, theoretically they are supposed to enhance our presentation. But the sad fact is that many presenters still think of visual aids only as PowerPoint, which they then use as crib sheets or a version of their speaker notes – something I truly hate.

Think about PowerPoint presentations – do they *really* enhance? Or do they actually get in the way of the personality of the speaker (almost always in my experience). Unless you have the time or energy to make your PowerPoint presentation dance and whistle I would be inclined to avoid it.

If you do want to use visual aids then use real ones. A former colleague of mine tells a story about starfish on a beach to illustrate the point that every small thing can make a difference. It goes like this: A mother and daughter were walking along the beach when a wave came in and deposited a load of starfish on the beach. The starfish were stranded and started dying. The little girl started picking up the starfish and throwing them back into the sea, one by one. The mother said 'What are you doing? You can't make a difference to all those starfish.' To which the little girl replied, 'No, but I'll make a big difference to this one.' At which point my colleague holds up a real starfish. Very powerful.

You could, for example, show copies of artwork, photographs, play a song and so on – much more powerful and meaningful than bullet-pointed sentences on a big screen.

So, begin by assuming you don't need PowerPoint and then add it when you do. Quite apart from anything else, the eyes absorb information faster than the ears (we read at around 230 words per minute and hear around 120 words per minute). Therefore, if we are presented with a conflict between listening and reading – we will read. However, if you do feel the need to use PowerPoint, here are some tips:

- Cut back on the number of slides: make each one earn its place.
- Top and tail yourself: begin with *no* visuals other than yourself.
- Use blank slides in between points so the audience focuses on you.
- Keep slides simple.
- Minimise words – maximise pictures/diagrams.
- Remember alternatives to visuals: the story, examples, anecdotes, analogies and so on.
- *Do not read out the slides!!!*

And, remember, the most powerful visual aid is *you*!

Questions
If handled badly, question sessions can very often scupper what was otherwise a perfectly good presentation or speech.

Here are some tips:
- Plan ahead (anticipate the likely questions and rehearse your answers).
- Don't criticise the question or the questioner.
- Acknowledge the right of the questioner to ask a question; for example, 'That's a fair/interesting/new/thought-provoking/stimulating question'.
- If you don't know – admit it, seek answers from others, say you will find out.
- Don't accept multiple questions if you can't handle them (and personally, as an audience member, I would always rather hear one question and one answer than try to keep track of multiple ones).
- Defer long answers to the end or afterwards.
- Don't meet hostile questions with hostility – keep calm.
- Feel free to ask for the question to be repeated.
- Take time to think (scribble the question on a piece of paper).
- Bridge from the negative to the positive (for example, 'That's a valid point; however, the real issue is...'; 'The question you should be asking is...'; 'It makes more sense to talk about...').

- Rephrase the question.
- Seek allies in the room: ask 'Who else thinks this way?'.
- Take questions at the end – get the audience to make notes.
- Finish on time – let others go – but you can stay behind to answer questions.
- Look at everyone as you answer, not just the questioner.
- In team presentations, agree in advance who will answer the questions or choose the presentation leader who will decide which team member answers which particular question.

And finally, don't worry too much about whether people liked you or not. The real test of an effective presentation is whether or not people do something differently as a result of it.

I used to run a residential leadership programme. In those days at the end of the programme we used to judge how successful it had been by the number and quality of the action points that our delegates had identified. On one particular occasion we had a speaker talking about individual learning. Almost without exception every delegate loathed him. They thought he was patronising, out of touch and a bit of a know-it-all. However, interestingly, at the end of the programme when we shared the action points, there were more actions around individual learning than any other topic on the entire course. He had got them so cross they were actually thinking about the topic. It was inadvertent, I must admit, as he did not intend such a negative response. But the point is that what they felt about him was not the most important measure of his effectiveness as a speaker. I am not saying you should annoy people, simply that the true test is in what happens afterwards.

Some critical dos and don'ts!

DO	DON'T
- **Make friends** - **Follow up with people with whom you bonded** - **Concentrate on the key things you want people to remember in presentations** - **Keep your presentations short and focused** - **Think about your audience**	- **Pretend to be interested in someone for the sake of it** - **Forget to share your networks with others** - **Give too much information** - **Try to look clever** - **Worry too much about whether people like you or not**

9 **Staying sane**

*The battles that count aren't the ones for the
gold medals. The struggles within yourself –
the invisible, inevitable battles inside all of us
– that's where it's at.*
Jesse Owens, Olympic gold medal athlete

Outcomes
After reading this chapter you will:
- **Know what causes you stress**
- **Identify some techniques for dealing with the pressure**

We've already identified that leadership at the top is a tough job, albeit with its own rewards. For many people the challenge is emotional and mental: keeping focused on the overall aims of the organisation while at the same time working with human beings who can be unpredictable, while still having to be conscious that we have an enormous effect on what goes on. All this can be very stretching.

You have to be acutely self-aware to be successful as a leader. But that acute self-awareness can also make us very sensitive to those things in ourselves that we don't like much. We become very conscious of our failures and failings and it can be very easy to let that awareness distort our self-image so that we forget that actually we're pretty alright as human beings. I can tell you from my own experience that those leaders who wake up in the middle of the night agonising about where they went wrong, who beat themselves up for their mistakes, who hold themselves accountable for what goes badly are often better than those leaders who drive along, blindly indifferent to the casualties along the roadside caused by their erratic driving!

On top of your own self-analysis, you also have an enormous job to do. You are responsible for an entire organisation and will be held accountable for its success or failure, even when circumstances have been greater than your ability to influence or respond to them. And that means it can be very stressful at the top.

This chapter is primarily about what you can do as an individual to manage your own stress levels and maintain a healthy and proportionate sense of self.

What is stress?
Stress is essentially a term used to describe the pressure that is being put upon us, either internally or externally. In itself it is not necessarily a bad thing – and

in fact we tend to call it 'pressure' or 'challenge' when we feel we can handle it and 'stress' when we feel we can't.

What makes the difference between whether we feel overwhelmed or challenged is largely due to our perception of what is happening to us. That is not to say that situations aren't in and of themselves intrinsically difficult. Of course they are. But how is it that some people fall apart under such circumstances, or get ill or distressed, while others appear perfectly well able to cope?

It's all about perception. Our ability to cope with stress is largely down to our perception of what is happening and our perception of our ability to deal with it.

In any aspect of our lives we have challenges which are accompanied by things we perceive as supports, and those we perceive as constraints. Constraints are those things that make us feel that the situation we are in is challenging or difficult. For example, we may be running out of funds for a particular project; we may not have the technology or resources we need; our people may be inexperienced, unskilled or unmotivated. Or we may have difficult relationships with some individuals in the organisation.

Supports are those things that we perceive as helping us. We may get a sudden influx of cash, or a new piece of equipment or a team that is working well together.

We will perceive ourselves as having stress not simply when the constraints are greater than the supports but also when the challenge feels bigger than our capacity to deal with it.

The diagram below illustrates what happens to us when supports and constraints are in conflict with one another. I unashamedly stole this from a friend of mine, John Edmondson, who is one of the best psychologists in the country and an expert at stress to boot.

The diagram speaks for itself. Obviously the best place to be is in the upper right quadrant. Having said that, however, recognise that you will not always be in the 'best' place. The trick is to notice where you are and to do something about moving (perhaps even literally!).

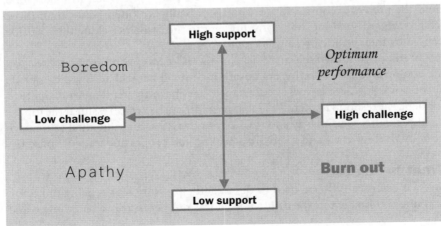

Stress is different for different people. What makes you feel challenged and excited may well cause other people real upset and difficulty. This is particularly important to recognise at the top of the organisation because it is too easy to forget that others may not be able to keep up with your vision and excitement. Further, even if you are experiencing high levels of stress, as the leader at the top you need to make sure that you are not passing on your stress to others around you.

When you are told that one of the qualities you need at the top is the ability to stay calm, that's not simply referring to your internal sense of calmness, but to your ability to disguise your stress levels from others around you. That sounds hard – and it is – but it is so important. Your role is about giving people hope and if they see you unable to cope, that will adversely affect their ability to cope themselves.

Having said all that, you are still a human being and so you need to find a way to manage and minimise your stress.

There are five main generic causes of stress:
1. Our perception of the demand placed upon us.
2. Our perception that there is no balance between the demand and the support.
3. Either one bit of our lives is taking up more time and attention than we want or another bit isn't getting enough time and attention.
4. We are asked to do something which challenges our intrinsic value set.
5. We are experiencing a period of major change – whether positive or negative.

How likely are you to get stressed?

You are more likely to experience unacceptable stress if there is not at least some balance in your life: some area in which you think things are going well. I know from experience that if things are tough at work, having a healthy life outside it really helps – and of course vice versa.

So, how do you feel about how well you are doing in all the key areas in your life (after all – you are not just a chief exec/senior manager!)? You will experience stress if there is an area that is important to you but which you do not feel is going well or on which you're not spending enough time. And at the top of the organisation it is very easy to let work dominate.

The following questionnaire is designed simply to get you to think about how happy you are overall. I have listed a few areas that typically matter to people. You may find you want to adjust the questionnaire to suit your own particular circumstance. However, the key thing here is to notice which areas are important and which are not, and how well you feel you are doing in them. If you mark something as relatively unimportant and you're not doing well at it – well so what? It's about getting some perspective and concentrating on those things that really matter.

Having said that, as your life moves and changes you will find that your priorities also change. For example, if you have fallen in love and are planning a future with someone, the chances are that this will become more important than work. Or if you are at a critical point in your career, or there is some major thing happening at work, then for a period of time that might be more important than family. Don't be unrealistic. Of course, ultimately, for most people, family comes first in the overall wider context, but for particular times in your life it is possible that you will need their patience and support while you concentrate on something else. I don't think there's anything wrong with that, provided that's not a permanent state of affairs and that you a) acknowledge their support and b) give your support back!

How do I feel about my life?

Rank the following life areas in order of importance from 1 (being the most important) and 11 (being the least important). Then mark on a score of 1 to 5 how satisfied you are with that part of your life (with 1 being not very satisfied and 5 being very satisfied). Below is a fictitious example of what the questionnaire might look like when completed.

Life area	How important is it to me?	How satisfied am I with it?	Action?
My job	3	4	
My relationships with my immediate colleagues	9	3	
The kind of organisation I work for	4	4	
The way my career is developing	6	2	Talk to my manager about new opportunities
My love life (emotional)	1	5	
My love life (physical)	11	3	
My family life	2	4	
My home (the physical environment)	7	2	Talk to hubby and kids about house-work rota
My social life	8	3	
Relationships with my friends	10	2	
My hobby or outside interest	5	1	Ring Nicky and ask if she wants to join me at the crochet club

The important point to note is discrepancies between the two figures. Are your scoring 3s, 4s and 5s in your satisfaction of those areas you ranked in importance from 1 to 6? If you are not scoring highly in those areas that really matter to you at the moment, then that is where you need to focus your attention.

You will notice that there is an action column – the point of that is that you don't just accept those areas where you feel you are not as happy or doing as well as you would like. You do something about it!

Recognising your own symptoms of stress

So how do you know if you are over-stressed? I said earlier that stress is different for different people. It is also true that each person's symptoms of stress are different. The test is to notice changes in your own behaviour (or changes in others' behaviour if you are monitoring their stress levels). For example, perhaps you are normally garrulous and excitable and you find yourself morose and silent; or you normally pick at your food and are now scoffing it down! It is the *change* in behaviour that is critical to notice.

Test your stress levels

Read each of the statements listed below and tick those that apply to you when you are under too much stress.

- [ ] I am easily irritated
- [ ] I have difficulty concentrating for any length of time
- [ ] I feel tired even when I wake up in the morning
- [ ] I have difficulty making even simple decisions
- [ ] The quality of my sleep deteriorates: I have difficulty getting to sleep and/ or I wake in the night
- [ ] I have difficulty controlling my temper
- [ ] I feel powerful negative emotions
- [ ] I feel generally run down and rather unwell
- [ ] Life seems to be hopeless; nothing seems worthwhile and I feel really low
- [ ] My eating pattern alters: I either lose my appetite or I seem to eat more food than usual
- [ ] I have difficulty absorbing new data
- [ ] I suffer from frequent headaches
- [ ] I have difficulty recalling information when I need to
- [ ] I drink more alcohol than usual
- [ ] I experience dramatic mood swings
- [ ] I miss or am late for appointments
- [ ] I feel wound up and unable to relax properly

- [ ] I am unable to achieve my normal level of creativity
- [ ] I suffer from backache regularly
- [ ] I feel inadequate and unable to cope
- [ ] I take time off work
- [ ] I suffer from indigestion
- [ ] I seem to lack capacity to focus on one thing at a time – my mind keeps wandering to other issues
- [ ] The smallest thing sends me into a panic
- [ ] I smoke more cigarettes than usual
- [ ] I have a frequent need to urinate
- [ ] In discussion with other people I frequently repeat myself
- [ ] My driving is erratic and my judgement impaired
- [ ] I seem to spend a lot of time worrying
- [ ] I feel lethargic and uninterested with work and/or life
- [ ] I find myself more frequently arguing with my partner/family/friends
- [ ] I find myself uninterested in things I previously liked

If you notice that your answers to these are giving you the message that you are under too much stress then you need to do something about it. Remember, your perception is the first thing that will help. It will always be stressful at the top – what you need to work on is how you view it.

We are our own worst enemy!

My friend I mentioned earlier, John Edmondson, talks about how as human beings we can be our own worst enemies.

He talks about what he calls dysfunctional assumptions. Those are assumptions about how we should be in the world that are unrealistic and unachievable. For example, we all want to be accepted. That is a functional way to think. However, it is dysfunctional if you want to be liked all the time by everyone. That's not possible and you need to accept it.

We all want to feel in control. However, we can't be in control of everything all the time. We all want to be competent. But inevitably we will make mistakes. We feel responsible for things. But we can only be responsible for what we do, not for what others do. We want to be in control of our emotions, but sometimes we will get angry and emotional and want to cry or shout.

The point is that we need to accept the fact that we are human beings and that we are not perfect. It sounds so obvious – but it is often so difficult for us to accept. We engage in thought processes that can make things worse for us.

Are you guilty of any of the following?

Awfulising

This is when we imagine the worst about a situation. You know, something goes wrong at work or a mistake is made. You immediately assume you'll get the sack. And you'll feel so bad about yourself that you won't be able to find another job. You'll end up defaulting on your mortgage and being made homeless. Your partner will leave you for someone else and you'll end up on the streets – drinking too much...Recognise any of this? And this all happens in about 0.2 of a second!

Action

- Give yourself a reality check: how likely is any of this to come to pass?!
- Focus on the moment you are in – not the moment that may or may not come!

Musterbating (should/must/ought)

This one of my favourite John Edmondson expressions: the rigid thinking. You know – things must be done right, people must do as they're told, they must meet deadlines, they must do a good job, they must not make mistakes and so on. The reality of the world is that people don't always do what they should, meet their deadlines or clean up their mistakes.

Action

- Allow for mistakes to happen.
- Look at what can be done to put it right or avoid it next time.
- Forgive, forgive, forgive!

Mind reading

This is where we imagine we know what people are thinking. We walk into a room of trustees and one of them appears to frown at us. We immediately assume that they've found out something and we're going to get into trouble!

Action

- Ask people outright what they are thinking.
- Question them in response to their body language if it appears to you to be negative.

Over-generalising

Over-generalising is about making something worse than it really is. We made a mistake and think that everyone is going to think that we're rubbish at everything. Or one small thing goes wrong and we extrapolate it into a complete disaster.

Action

- Give yourself a reality check.
- Get a sense of perspective: how will you feel in a week, a month, ten years, on your death bed – will it really matter then?

Underestimating our skills

This is an absolute classic. Marcus Aurelius once said something which is commonly quoted in its modern form as 'Never let the future disturb you. You will meet it, if you have to, with the same weapons of reason which today arm you against the present.' We didn't get to where we are today without having the ability to solve problems and, whatever we are faced with, we will still be able to deal with it. Honest!

Action
- Remind yourself of how you have dealt successfully with similar situations before.
- Trust your abilities.

Focusing on how we feel, not what we do

As human beings we are driven by our emotions. We are conscious of our reactions to things, we know how we feel inside. And this can very often make us forget about the fact that no one knows how we are feeling unless we show them. For example, chances are that if you are nervous giving a public presentation, no one even notices and you do a good job anyway. How you feel is not the issue here, it's what you do. You can do a great job and be terrified. The great job is the bit that matters!

Action
- Concentrate on what you are doing not how you are feeling.

Forgetting to solve the problem

Another classic. We get so wrapped up in how awful it is we forget that we can do something about it. *Our latest communication with staff has been horribly misinterpreted.* Well, go and communicate again and get it right this time. *Our trustees have gone nuts over something we did without checking with them first* – well, go and clean it up.

Action
- Solve the blooming problem – change the situation.
- And if you can't solve it – accept it.

Reinforcing our misery

This is when we focus on all the things that are bad, or we do things that contribute to that bad feeling. A lovely example is my friend Deborah. She was having a dinner party and rang me up, late in the afternoon, horribly stressed and in tears saying she couldn't cope and could I please come over and help out. I arrived to discover that she had really loud techno music blasting out throughout the house. Nothing wrong with that – but I doubt it was contributing to a sense of calmness and well-being!

Action
- Make sure that you are not adding to the problem by doing things that make it worse.
- Ask for help.

Tips for keeping a sense of perspective

I think that, of all of the many pieces of useful advice that can be given about staying sane and relatively stress-free, the most useful is about keeping a sense of perspective. The following tips should help you to achieve that.

If you are in a difficult situation that is causing you worry then change the way you see it:

- Write down the thing that is causing you stress.
- Write down how it is making you feel.
- Write down how your feelings are influencing your behaviour and your ability to gain some perspective.
- Ask yourself the question: 'What is the worst thing that could happen?'
- Then ask yourself : 'If the worst happens, what can you do?'
- Ask yourself: 'How likely is it that the worst thing will happen?'
- Then ask yourself: 'What is most likely to happen?'

If you do this you will probably find that the situation is not nearly as bad as it seems at the time. Remember the words of Corrie Ten Boom: 'Worry does not empty tomorrow of its sorrow, it empties today of its strength.'

Build up and use a strong personal support network

Make sure you have support mechanisms in place to help you to deal with difficult times. You must not try to be over-dependent or too self-reliant. Talking to someone about what is bothering you can often help you to see the wood for the trees and put things into perspective. Bottling up emotion rarely helps and can often make things worse.

Ensure you have plenty of people to whom you can go to meet your various needs. And I do mean more than one. I've always found it odd how, right up until the point that we fall in love, we have plenty of people in our lives who meet our needs – those who we have fun with, those who are very practical and help us fix things, those who sympathise with us. And then, suddenly, we fall in love and expect all these needs to be met by one person, putting unacceptable pressure on them and setting them up to fail! And we wonder why our relationships go wrong! Don't take it out at home. It's not fair and, not only that, they have their lives too and want you to concentrate on them, not your woes.

Fill in the following table and if you find it's only one or two names, have another think. If you are always using the same people you will usually get the same answers!

	Name
Who can I rely on in a crisis?	
Who makes me feel good about myself?	
Who can I be totally myself with?	
Who can give me honest feedback in a way that I can accept?	
Who can I talk to when I am worried about work?	
Who can I talk to when I am worried about home?	
Who is able to make me stop and think about what I am doing?	
Who helps me put things into perspective?	
Who is good fun to be with?	
Who helps me take my mind off things?	
Who introduces me to new people/ideas/opportunities?	
Who can give me honest feedback in a way that I can accept?	
Who is able to make me stop and think about what I am doing?	

Use your support network regularly – not just in times of crisis.

Deal with the problem

For any stressor there is normally a cause or an event which may or may not be within your control. The first thing to do is to see if you can remove the cause of the stress. For example, if you get stressed about the fact that trains are frequently late, you're probably heading for trouble!

If you can't remove the cause then you need to find a way to detach yourself from it. So if on your list there are things over which you have no control, then don't worry about them – accept them and move on.

The meditative stuff

Quiet reflection and meditation doesn't work for everyone. However, there are some quick, simple things you can do to get yourself back into control in those immediate short-term moments of stress that can be difficult to deal with.

Here are a couple of techniques to help you to gather yourself together quickly before you react.

Focusing outside the moment
Go to a window or a door, or look at a picture or a plant. Really look at it, focus on it, the colour, the shape, the texture – continue to look at it until you feel your heart rate slowing down, your breathing becoming more measured.

Going to the quiet place
Close your eyes and imagine that you are walking through a door. Outside the door is a large field full of tall waving grass. You are walking through the grass, the sun is shining and there is a gentle breeze. The grass begins to gradually thin and you come to a small gently trickling stream. There is a pleasantly shady spot under a willow tree on the bank with a soft mossy base. You sit down on the moss which feels spongy and comfortable. You close your eyes and feel the gentle breeze on your face and in your hair, a soft warmth from the sun on your skin and you hear the whisper of the leaves on the trees and the trickling of the stream. You feel peaceful, calm and safe.

This is just a trick for you – you can imagine your own place.

Five-stage plan for dealing with stress
This is a simple way of pulling together what we have talked about so far.

1. Understanding and acceptance of self
- Accept that you are human and will make mistakes.
- Learn your own values and priorities.
- Accept your limitations.
- Recognise your stressors.
- Focus on your strengths.

I know not all that may be coming, but be it what it will, I'll go to it laughing.
Herman Melville, *Moby-Dick*

2. Tackle the problem
- Identify the stressor.
- Attempt to change it.
- If you're unable to change it – accept it.
- If you're unable to accept it – move on.

Grant me the serenity to accept the things I cannot change, the courage to change the things I can, and the wisdom to know the difference.
Reinhold Niebuhr, 'The Serenity Prayer'

3. Self-nurturing

- Treat yourself to things you like doing.
- Look after your physical well-being.
- Spend time with people who make you feel good.

No one can make you feel inferior without your consent.

Attributed to Eleanor Roosevelt

4. Emotional expression

- Develop a support network.
- Engage in two-way conversations with your manager.
- Accept that the appropriate expression of emotion is fine.
- Maintain a sense of humour.

No matter how strong an individual is, we have to live as a human community.

The 14th Dalai Lama

5. Active distraction or quiet reflection

- Do something at the end of each day to mark the distinction between home and work.
- Do something that requires mental effort so that you can't think about what is stressing you (for example, play chess, read a book or play a sport).
- Take some time to give yourself mental space.

Silence is the element in which great things fashion themselves together; that at length they may emerge, full-formed and majestic, into the daylight of Life, which they are thenceforth to rule.

Thomas Carlyle, *Sartor Resartus*

Finally remember these two things. First, as Mary Pickford said:

'Failure' is not the falling down, but the staying down.

and, second...

Worse things happen at sea!

Some critical dos and don'ts!

DO

- Keep a sense of perspective
- Build up a support network
- Remember that you are a human being
- Focus on what you can do rather than how you feel
- Maintain a sense of humour

DON'T

- Let one aspect of your life dominate for too long
- Forget to use your support network
- Beat yourself up for making mistakes
- Forget to solve the problem
- Lose sight of what really matters

10 The gift to see us as others see us

One of the most important things that has helped me in my personal leadership journey is learning from the experience of others. Why make a whole new mistake yourself if you can avoid it by finding out how someone else handled it? So this chapter is full of personal reflections of other CEOs in the sector: the advice they would give their younger selves; what they have learned is important and those things they think are useful for you to know. I haven't edited them at all – so you hear their voices in what they say. Some are short and to the point; others are more reflective in style. But the one thing they all have in common is that they have been there, made the mistakes and learned along the way. Indeed, Paul Streets, whose thoughts you will come across later, told me that writing these things down felt almost cathartic for him. I thought that was a great idea. So perhaps you should write down your own top tips to yourself – you'll be amazed at how wise you actually are! I hope you find the following thoughts as inspiring and useful as I did.

In no particular order:

Jan McLoughlin, Director General, PDSA

- Go back to the 'root cause': when I feel removed I go back to one of our Pet Hospitals for the day, see the good work we do to help people and pets, and remind myself what it's all about.
- Don't rush decisions: take advice from those who've been there before. You don't always know what you don't know.
- Be prepared to walk the 'field of broken glass': things won't always be perfect, but that's okay.
- Spend time establishing a good relationship and clear ground rules with your chair and trustees – it will pay dividends in the long run.
- Remember, no matter how bad your 'bad hair day' is, people take their lead from you as their leader; you are always on display and so have to be mindful of how you're coming across.

Andy Garnett, Founder, The Garnett Foundation

- People like achieving things; structure work so people can achieve things linked to their skills, attitude and application:
  1. every day;
  2. every week;
  3. every month;
  4. and every year.

- Celebrate those achievements, learn from them and communicate them.
- Don't waste time trying to get people to achieve things they obviously can't. (Don't try and teach a pig to sing.)
- Invest in success.
- The customer is not always right, but still needs to be treated as a customer.
- Connect ideas and involve people in those connections.
- Having a problem is no problem, denying you have it creates the difficulty.

Beverley Costa, CEO, Mothertongue

- Don't listen to old fogies who try to give you advice. It is all very sensible and they are right when they say that the answer to your regular question of 'How hard can that be?', when faced with a challenge that requires a completely new skill set, is 'Very hard'. But if you had listened to them you wouldn't have done anything.
- Mistakes are your friends. Shame, humiliation and embarrassment are not. You can learn, have some fun and embrace these friends.
- When you can't find the way through, stop looking and start listening.
- Find people who can do the things you can't and enjoy their ability.
- Keep an eye on that old ego. Know when enough is enough.

Peter Wanless, CEO, NSPCC

- As a leader you are on display at all times. People will draw energy (or the opposite – take over the apathy) from how you present yourself.
- The acquisition of greater authority doesn't automatically make you wiser and worth listening to. Leadership does not equal you deciding the outcome of every dispute and discussion. It is far better to create an environment in which many others can do that for themselves with confidence.
- Pressure can be a good thing because it faces you up to doing the very best you can. If it feels tough – it is, but others have placed confidence in you to lead them through this. If it were all straightforward you wouldn't be needed. (Constantly have to tell myself this one!)
- It costs nothing to be civilised with others and if you think someone is behaving badly, pick them up on it.
- Surround yourself with people you trust and respect. Make sure they know that (and are deserving of it).

Henny Braund, CEO, Anthony Nolan Trust

- Listen a lot but be prepared to filter. The most eager to tell you how 'it is', aren't necessarily quite right.
- Trust your instincts, there is a huge benefit to being new. Write down your first impressions and then look back at them within a month, you'll be amazed how right you were.

- Be bold and just get on with it, do not procrastinate, it's easier to sort things out early on when you're less emotionally attached plus you'll get those early wins.
- Be visible.
- Believe in yourself, they wouldn't have appointed you if they didn't think you could do the job.
- Take food on your first day. I nearly passed out from hunger as 'lunch' somehow got omitted from my induction...
- Make friends with your PA. They are essential to your success.

Catherine Johnstone CBE, former CEO, Samaritans

- Accept that you don't need to be the one that has all the answers. Surround yourself with good people and allow them to shine.
- Always have a plan and share it with all the people who need to contribute. Ideally, share the development of the plan so people feel ownership.
- Remember why you chose to work in the charity sector and focus on who we are here to serve.
- Invest in your trustees, and if possible be one yourself. Executive leadership and trustee leadership must complement each other and when this happens your organisation flies.
- Remember to make every penny count – we are largely investing public money which is a privilege.

Jane Gurney, CEO, Essex and Herts Air Ambulance Trust

- Trust your gut instincts.
- Always have absolute belief and passion for your cause!
- Don't ignore the little things as they can quickly become the big things.
- Keep your sense of humour (you're going to need it!).
- Don't forget to stop and celebrate the successes along the way.

Caron Bradshaw, CEO, Charity Finance Group

- You will make mistakes, you will fall down but, as best put by this quote, 'the greatest glory in living lies not in never falling but in rising every time we fall'.
- Make time for the things that fill you up with joy and laughter – they are too important not to prioritise – they give you the resources to deal with the difficult stuff.
- Things always feel more difficult and intense from the inside looking out – others looking in from outside will see it very differently.
- Don't take your work on holiday – take proper breaks. If you are doing it right your staff should be able to handle things in your absence.
- In order to enjoy rainbows you have to endure rain! Bad stuff happens but it just makes the good stuff that much sweeter and there will nearly always be something good that comes from a bad patch/challenges.

Alistair Mortimer, VP, Bank of America Merrill Lynch

■ Not everyone shares your own motivations and abilities – celebrate the differences. When I was younger I could be very hard on those who I thought weren't performing well, or who weren't 'pulling their weight'. I have become a bit more subtle and thoughtful over time. While sometimes it's fine to ask people to 'up their game', it's often not, because the individual might be more effective working in a different way. Also, while you might be very driven and always be prepared to go the extra mile, or work that extra hour, that's because of your own motivations and it just may not be fair to ask for that same commitment from everyone else. That's not an acceptance of defeat, it's an acceptance of reality.

■ It's okay to be open, but sometimes you can be too open. When you're starting out you can generally get away with being very open and transparent, particularly about your feelings in the workplace. Unfortunately, although we'd like to think we can continue to do that throughout the remainder of our careers, that's just not always going to be possible. Particularly if you have senior responsibilities, there can be many situations where it's simply not appropriate or sensible (or even legal!) to openly communicate your true feelings on every issue. For someone like myself, who finds it very hard to hide my feelings – and frustrations! – this can be incredibly difficult, and it's actually something that you may have to practice.

■ It's about the ethos, not the role. It has taken me a while to learn that the specifics of a job are really not as important as the culture and environment around the job. The details of what you're doing will change, and that's necessary, but what will drive your success at the role, and ultimately your fulfilment, is how well you understand and fit into the culture of the place in which you work. That takes time and effort – you need to expend energy learning about your environment, finding out who does what, and how the organisation reacts to issues, particularly serious ones. It can be easy to turn a blind eye on occasion (for example, you don't really like the values of a place, but you figure you need the salary and you convince yourself it doesn't matter) but that rarely ends well in the long run.

■ Keep looking upwards and outwards. Having additional perspective is never wrong for a number of reasons. It's very easy to get one's head down and worry about the specific tasks that need to be performed, but if you lift your gaze above the parapet occasionally you'll be more effective, happier and, ironically, more engaged. Some examples include: understanding how things are done elsewhere; following what's happening more generally in your sector/area; making sure your energies are also used and replenished in other spaces outside work; having a mentor outside your workplace; and occasionally seeking advice from friends and family on work-related issues. Oh, and do use your holiday entitlements!

- But sometimes, it just really IS tough at the top. As a senior leader it can indeed be tough and lonely, and it's natural to try and make yourself feel better. Many leaders will do that by sharing their concerns with colleagues, and that is fine within limits. However, actually sometimes tough decisions just have to be taken, by you on your own, without enough information, and with the risk that things might go wrong and it will be your fault if they do! Don't be tempted to try and devolve the responsibility to a wider group in every case, unless that's genuinely the right thing to do. The feeling when you've got it wrong is hard to deal with, but you have to consider the sense of achievement you'll experience when you get it right, and your leadership has been fundamental to the success of the organisation and its objectives.

Gerry Lejeune OBE, CEO, Berkshire Community Foundation

- You don't have to be an expert at everything but surround yourself with people who are.
- Make sure you meet with all your organisation (however big) at least once a year.
- Remember: it is nice to be important – but more important to be nice.
- Remember to say thank you to your supporters and volunteers no matter how busy you are.
- Remember work/life balance – no one in the graveyard ever wishes they spent more time in the office.
- Have fun and don't be afraid to tell people how amazing they are and how proud you feel of your organisation and people who work with you.

Ray Lock, CEO, Forces In Mind Trust
My five top tips for my younger self (not that I'd have listened to an old windbag like me)

In common with everyone in the Armed Forces, I joined at the lowest possible rank – in my case Acting Pilot Officer. Given the importance of leadership to successful military endeavour, it wasn't a surprise to be given so much leadership education; but it was odd to be confronted first hand on quite so many occasions with examples of just plain poor leadership. So by the time I got my hands on a relatively senior position, I had a clear view of: my own strengths and weaknesses; what worked for me and what didn't; how people saw me; and how I viewed others – this last point would fill a book on false prejudice and mis-preconception in its own right.

The best rehearsed yet least valid preconception is that military and civilian senior leadership are somehow chalk and cheese; and that the act of transition from one to the other is an elusive alchemy of turning lead into gold. Well they're not, they're exactly the same (if you ignore the bombing/bayoneting/fishing part). Because:

- You probably do know better.
- Listening creates expectation.
- Forget what you did, remember what you learned.

- How you speak about your boss, is how your team will speak about you.
- Enjoy your time in post, you are a tenant not an owner.

I made my worst mistakes when I failed to trust my own instincts – why didn't I? I had greater and more relevant experience and training; so having weighed everything up, why then listen to the siren voices? **I probably did know better**. And when you do listen to your team, it's easy to generate in them the false beliefs either that you are going to do what they suggest, or that you are somehow miraculously going to deliver the truly impossible. **Simply by listening, you've created expectation**.

One drawback of a meritocracy is that everyone thinks they could do their previous, and more junior, job better than the current incumbent. Possibly that's true, but rare is the person (and I'm certainly not one) who can take for long the drone of the 'when I was' leader. Circumstance will always have changed – not least because the leaders themselves have. **Sharing what you learned, and saving what you did for the pub**, offers the badge of humility only others can bestow, and which all the good leaders wear. Indeed, who am I really to judge the leadership of others? But if I criticize them, openly, I encourage others to criticize me in a similar way. Is that helpful? Probably not: you live by the sword, you die by the sword. If you're **disparaging about your boss, your team will disparage you**.

Could all the lows that my younger self endured have been avoided had I been armed with these piercing insights? They might have been shallower certainly; but then organisations have amazing powers of recuperation, and obstinate resistance to change. Understanding that I didn't own an organisation, nor ever the people within it, only really came to me as I handed on to the next leader. To develop and to cherish, as well as to deliver: each has value of its own. **Always a tenant, never an owner**.

And a bonus sixth top tip: if there's the slightest doubt, even the tiniest inkling of doubt – **don't press 'Send'**!

Barbara Gelb, CEO, Together for Short Lives
Five things I would tell my younger self

- Do that Master's degree sooner rather than later. I waited about five years from the time of first becoming a CEO before I launched into it. It was the best thing I ever did and also the toughest. Really helped me to understand the challenges of the role in a theoretical perspective and gave me a lot of confidence in arguing my corner. It helped me to understand complexity in the world that we inhabit in the charitable sector and the immense value of being able to sit with uncertainty in our work, and the limitations of jumping to certainty.
- Get a mentor and a coach. Both have their place. I engaged in coaching for the first time when I had been a CEO for ten years. Coaching has helped me hugely with growing my self-belief and in so doing has enabled me to drive forward in taking the organisation to greater heights. It is only recently that I have secured the support of a mentor. Why did I

not do this before? Mentoring is an opportunity to get support from an experienced peer CEO with the challenges that one faces, in a risk-free and confidential space.

- Also create a peer network. Don't get so bogged down in the day job that you don't have time for connecting with others in similar roles and from whom you can draw support. This will feed and energise you and you will bring even more back into your role as a consequence. Again, to be honest I don't feel I have done enough to prioritise this over the years. And if I had my time again I would do lots of it. And plan to do much more of it going forward now.

- Get out there and see how others are doing it. One of the most helpful things we have done recently as a senior team is to get out and ask some admired organisations how they do things. I have learnt loads and gained lots of new ideas to bring back into our charity so that we can make things better.

- Become a mentor. Don't underestimate the experience that you are building up as a CEO and create the opportunity to become a mentor quite early on. I have neglected to do this, to my cost quite honestly. I am now about to launch into becoming a mentor to a new charity CEO and am really excited about it. I know that it will help me to consolidate my experience and knowledge about being a charity CEO and will enable me to bring loads back into my role in our charity.

Jamie Wilcox, Head of Volunteer Services and Patient Experience, Great Ormond Street Hospital
Four key points I would give to my younger self

- **Boundaries**: don't try to be everyone's friend. Sometimes you just need to make decisions that are necessary and not everyone will like them. Although people will be angry/feel neglected/think you are favouring others, they will eventually understand and will more often than not respect you for your decision-making. They will certainly not thank you or admire you if you dither and try to appease everyone – it won't work!

- **Listen well**: be a good listener and take on board other people's ideas. No good trying to do everything yourself. Listen to what others have to say to help you make the right decisions.

- **Expertise**: remember that you can't be the expert in everything. But you can surround yourself with people who are. Rely on them and trust them to lead on their speciality. Encourage them to grow and become strong leaders.

- **Perspective**: remember everyone has a different perspective. Their perspective is not wrong, it's just different from yours. To avoid 'group think', always try to look at any issue, solution or opportunity from a range of different perspectives.

Cath Lee, CEO, Leeds Mencap
What I would have liked my younger self to know:

- Feel confident about who you are and the CEO this makes you. Other people's expectations of what a CEO should be like can sometimes lead you to adopt a style that is an uncomfortable fit. Adapt communication and management style to different people's needs or different situations but be yourself too.
- Don't assume anything and ask your team not to make assumptions about actions taken, knowledge or communication. Check understanding.
- Trustees are part of the team – manage them and support them to help them do their best to manage and support you.
- You will constantly have 'full brain syndrome'. Think of it as a rainmaker toy – constantly sifting ideas and sorting into different layers of priority or topics. It might feel a mess in there but you could think of it as 'a real durable (musical) instrument, colourful beads cascading, creating fascination' and, if you're lucky enough, your brain might have a 'colourful spinner for additional fun effects'.
- Make time to reflect on the good bits – your team members are amazing, talented people from whom you can learn and get support and encouragement; at the end of the day your efforts will have made something or someone's life better – that's not a bad job to be in!

Epilogue: so are you any good?

How do you judge whether or not you're doing a good job? How do you know whether or not you're an effective chief exec or senior person?

Is it the size of the balance sheet? Is it that you've grown the organisation or kept it small and focused? Is it that your trustees think you're good? Or that your staff do? Or your beneficiaries/service users? Is it that you've attracted funding, or built up huge reserves? Or that you've spent the reserves wisely and well on delivering the organisation's objectives? Are you managing the assets well – or selling them off because they're a distraction from the real work of the charity? Are you well known? Are you influencing national policy – or keeping focused locally? Any one of these things could be valid measures of your success.

Some will say the only test of your leadership is if you delivered the organisation's objectives. But does that make you good if, in doing that, you sacrificed your people, treated them unfairly or that in your ruthless determination to achieve the results you overlooked the human context? It's not that simple, is it?

Here's the thing. Different people will have different perceptions about how successful you are as a chief exec. So who's right? Well all of them and none of them. Whether you're lauded or lambasted, feted or fired, at the end of the day the only one who can really judge is you.

The *only* real test is if you can look deep into your heart, face yourself in the mirror and be able to say: 'I hung on to my integrity. I didn't hold anything back. I gave it my all. I did the best that I was able. I was courageous and humble.'

And in the end, can you say, 'My soul is intact'?

Chief execs' checklist of key questions

- Do you have a performance management system?
- Do you have a clear vision? Has this been communicated?
- Do you have a strategy for delivering your vision? Is it written down? Is there a clearly understood plan to achieve it?
- Do you meet at least monthly with your senior team?
- Do you have a clearly defined set of values with associated 'behavioural measurements'?
- Do you meet with your chair at least monthly?
- Do you delegate authority down the organisation?
- Do you have a strategy for raising funds?
- Does your senior team prepare and monitor its own budgets and performance?
- Do you have an effective mechanism for communicating with staff? Volunteers? Beneficiaries? Trustees?
- Do you regularly update your funders on your progress?
- Do you have ways of measuring how effective your organisation's work is?
- Do you regularly network with other chief execs and key players in your field of work?
- Do you regularly review the structure of the organisation to ensure that it is right for the present and the future?
- Do you ensure that you have access to the professional expertise you need (for example, charity law, employment law or finance)?
- Have you trained your managers in management and leadership skills?
- Do you plan in time to think?
- Are you keeping up with changes in the wider context in which you operate?
- Are you happy?

A voluntary sector aptitude test for chief executives

The Chief Executive of The Horse Trust, Jeanette Allen, while she was CEO of MedicAlert, shared a variation of this with me and I thought it was so amusing I've included an abridged version, hoping that it will make you smile too!

Do you have what it takes to be a chief exec?

1. Can you fake a smile convincingly all day long?
2. Can you read a paragraph and make it sound as if you've read the whole thing?
3. Can you use your fingers to add up and take away, without anyone noticing?
4. Can you draw a line, stick to it, then move it and pretend it was there all along?
5. Can you look as if you're listening even when you're miles away?
6. Can you manage an agenda so that the stuff that will make your trustees mad doesn't have enough time allocated to it?
7. Can you use Google?
8. Can you convince someone that you recognise them even though you haven't got a clue who they are and suspect you don't remember them because you didn't want to?
9. Can you fool people into believing you know what you're talking about?
10. Can you call a plumber?

References

Page xi – **Introduction epigraph:** This quote is attributed to Scott Simmerman, US management consultant; however, it appears to have been adapted from Joseph Joubert's quote 'Children have more need for models than critics' (translated from Joubert, Joseph (1895), *Pensées, essais, maximes et correspondance de J. Joubert*, Raynal, Paul Chaudru de (ed.), V. Le Normant, Paris)

Page xii – **George Bernard Shaw quote:** This text is popularly quoted in one but is a mixture of 'Epistle Dedicatory to Arthur Bingham Walkley' from *Man and Superman* (Shaw, G. B. (1903), *Man and Superman*, A. Constable & Co., Westminster, pp. xxxi–ii) and a speech made at Municipal Technical College and School of Art, Brighton, in 1907 (first printed in 'Art and Public Money', *Sussex Daily News*, 7 March 1907)

Page xii – **Theodore Roosevelt quote:** Roosevelt, Theodore (1910), 'The Man In The Arena', *Citizenship in a Republic* speech at the Sorbonne, Paris

Page 1 – **Chapter 1 epigraph:** Shakespeare, William (1903), *Henry V*, Blackie and Son Ltd, London, p. 61, IV. Prologue. 35–6

Page 4 – **Richard Olivier book:** Olivier, Richard (2003), *Inspirational Leadership: Henry V and the Muse of Fire – Timeless insights from Shakespeare's greatest leader*, Spiro Press

Page 5 – **William Shakespeare quote:** Shakespeare, William (1903), *Henry V*, Blackie and Son Ltd, London, p. 70, IV. I. 228–35

Page 7 – **Rudyard Kipling quote:** Kipling, Rudyard (1910), 'If', *Rewards and Fairies*, Doubleday, Garden City, New York, p. 175

Page 9 – **Chapter 2 epigraph:** The quote has been attributed to both Robert Quillen, American journalist and Robert Frost, American poet

Page 10 – **Definition of 'leadership':** Kouzes, James and Posner, Barry (1993), *Credibility: How leaders gain and lose it, why people demand it*, Jossey-Bass, San Francisco, p. 1

Page 17 – **Action-centred leadership:** See Adair, John (1973), *Action-Centred Leadership*, McGraw-Hill, London

Page 18 – **Key activities table:** The table is reproduced from Smith, Edwin Percy and Chase, Colin (1989), *The Manager as a Leader (Notes for Managers)*, Industrial Society Press

Page 25 – **Chapter 3 epigraph:** The quote has been attributed to Antoine de Saint-Exupéry; it is believed to have been derived from a text in Saint-Exupéry's book *Citadelle* (translated in English as *The Wisdom of the Sands*)

Page 25 – **The quote on vision:** This quote and its variations are attributed to Helen Keller and are believed to have originated from her comment made to a question 'What is worse than being born blind?'

Page 26 – **'Voltaire's' quote:** If you happen to know where this quote is from do get in touch!

Page 31 – **John F. Kennedy quote:** Kennedy, John F. (1961), excerpt from the 'Special Message to the Congress on Urgent National Needs', May 24, Section IX: Space

Page 35 – **Chapter 4 epigraph:** Whyte, William Hollingsworth (1950), 'Is Anybody Listening?', *Fortune*, September, p. 174

Page 37 – **Andrew Marr Quote:** Marr, Andrew (2004), *My Trade: A short history of British journalism*, Pan Books, pp. 183–4

Page 37 – **The quote on behaviour:** The quote is widely attributed to Peter F. Drucker, US management consultant, although its origin is unconfirmed

Page 49 – **Henry David Thoreau quote:** Thoreau, Henry David (1863), 'Life Without Principle', *The Atlantic Monthly*, vol. 12, no. 71, pp. 484–95

Page 51 – **Roger McGough poem:** McGough, Roger (1985), 'The Leader', *Sky in the Pie*, Puffin Books

Page 55 – **Chapter 5 epigraph:** The quote is widely attributed to Paul 'Bear' Bryant, American college football coach

Page 56 – **Definition of a 'real team':** Hackman, Richard (ed.) (1990), *Groups that work (and those that don't): Creating conditions for effective teamwork*, Jossey-Bass, San Francisco

Page 56 – **An overview of the Hay Group study:** See Hackman, Richard and Wageman, Ruth in partnership with Hay Group (2005), *Top Teams: Why some work and some do not* [working paper PDF], Hay Group Inc., available at www.haygroup.com/Downloads/uk/misc/
Top_Teams_Working_Paper_UK.pdf [accessed 19 October 2016]

Page 64 – **Research on group conformity:** See classic works on conformity by Asch, Solomon, (1951), 'Effects of group pressure upon the modification and distortion of judgment' in Guetzkow, Harold (ed.), *Groups, leadership and men*, Carnegie Press, Pittsburgh; Kelman, Herbert (1958), 'Compliance, identification, and internalization: Three processes of attitude change', *Journal of Conflict Resolution*, vol. 2, no. 1, pp. 51–60; and Milgram, Stanley (1974), *Obedience to authority: An experimental view*, HarperCollins. For a detailed overview of the subject also see Forsyth, Donelson, R. (1990), *Group Dynamics*, Brooks/Cole Publishing Company

Page 69 – **Emotional intelligence:** Goleman, Daniel (2005), *Emotional Intelligence: Why it can matter more than IQ*, Bantam Books

Page 73 – **Chapter 6 epigraph:** This quote is adapted from Desai, Bhadra (1960), *Indira Gandhi: Call to Greatness,* Popular Prakashan, Bombay, p. 71. In the book Indira recalls her grandfather Motilal's advice to her. The full quote is: 'There are two kinds of people, those who do the work and those who take the credit. Belong to the first category. Since not only do things get balanced, but there is also much less competition.'

Page 97 – **Chapter 7 epigraph:** This quote and its variations have been attributed to Dr William Edwards Deming, American academic and management consultant.

Page 98 – **Sigmoid Curve:** See Handy, Charles (1994), *The Age of the Paradox,* Harvard Business School Press, Boston; and Handy, Charles (2002), 'Elephants and Fleas: Is Your Organization Prepared for Change?', *Leader to Leader,* no. 24 (spring)

Page 101 – **Kriss Akabusi quote:** Akabusi, Kriss with Hartley, Tricia (2006), *Success comes in Cans: Learning Lessons for Life,* Network Continuum Education, p. 60

Page 103 – **The Moses metaphor:** See Bridges, William and Mitchell, Susan (2000), 'Leading Transition: A New Model for Change', *Leader to Leader,* no. 16 (spring). Also see Bridges, William (2006), *Getting Through The Wilderness. A Leader's Guide to Transition* [PDF], William Bridges & Associates, available at www.wmbridges.com/pdf/getting-thru-wilderness-2006-v2.pdf [accessed 22 October 2016]

Page 107 – **Chapter 8 epigraph:** Milne, A. A. (1985), *The Complete Winnie-the-Pooh and The House at Pooh Corner,* E. P. Dutton, New York, p. 288

Page 107 – **Eleanor Roosevelt quote:** Roosevelt, Eleanor (1960), *You Learn by Living,* Westminster John Knox

Page 108 – **Checklist of networking:** Inspired by Warren, Eve and Gielnik, Caroline (1995), *Empower Yourself: Self development for women,* Universities Press

Page 116 – **Speed of reading and hearing:** See Trauzettel-Klosinski, Susanne and Dietz, Klaus (2012), 'Standardized Assessment of Reading Performance: The New International Reading Speed Texts IreST', *Investigative Ophthalmology and Visual Science,* vol. 53, no. 9; and Wong, Linda (2014), *Essential Study Skills,* Cengage Learning

Page 119 – **Chapter 9 epigraph:** Owens, Jesse with Neimark, Paul (1970), *Blackthink: My life as a black man and a white man,* William Morrow and Company Inc., p. 150

Page 120 – **John Edmondson:** John is a consultant behavioural psychotherapist working in independent practice since 1995. As well as being a clinician in cognitive behavioural therapy (CBT) and eye movement desensitisation and reprocessing (EMDR) he has lectured in the UK and

Europe on a range of subjects including coaching and mentoring, stress in the workplace, bullying and harassment, and influencing skills

Page 126 – **Marcus Aurelius quote:** The original quote is 'Let not future things disturb thee, for thou wilt come to them, if it shall be necessary, having with thee the same reason which now thou usest for present things.'; Marcus Aurelius (1862), *The Thoughts of The Emperor Marcus Aurelius Antoninus,* (translated by Long, George), Little, Brown and Co., Boston, Book VII, p. 102

Page 127 – **Corrie Ten Boom quote:** Ten Boom, Corrie (1984), *Clippings from my Notebook,* World Wide Publications, Minneapolis, p. 33

Page 129 – **Herman Melville quote:** Melville, Herman (1851), *Moby-Dick,* Richard Bentley, London, p. 188

Page 129 – **The Serenity Prayer:** The full text of the prayer is believed to have originated from a sermon written by an American theologian, Reinhold Niebuhr. It was subsequently adopted, adapted and is still used by many religious and secular groups.

Page 130 – **Quote on self-nurturing:** This quote is widely attributed to Eleanor Roosevelt and is believed to have been crafted from public comments made by the first lady

Page 130 – **The Dalai Lama quote:** 14th Dalai Lama (2001), *Live in a Better Way. Reflections on Truth, Love and Happiness,* (Singh, Renuka (ed.)), Viking Compass, p. 90

Page 130 – **Thomas Carlyle quote:** Carlyle, Thomas (1840), *Sartor Resartus,* James Munroe, Boston, Book III, Chapter III, p. 221

Page 130 – **Mary Pickford quote:** Pickford, Mary (1935), *Why not Try God?,* H. C. Kinsey & Company, Inc., p. 33

Page 134 – **Final bullet point under Andy Garnett's tips:** See John Cleese's motivational speech; Cleese, John (1988), 'The Importance of Mistakes' at British-American Chamber of Commerce, Los Angeles

Page 135 – **Quote under Caron Bradshaw's tips:** This quote has been attributed to various authors, including Confucius, Irish writer Oliver Goldsmith and, in more recent times, Nelson Mandela who used these words during his 1998 visit to the US

Recommended reading

Anderson, James and Marilyn Ricci (eds), *Society & Social Science*, 1994, Open University Press

Chait, Richard P., William P. Ryan and Barbara E. Taylor, *Governance as Leadership*, 2005, John Wiley & Sons

Cook, Liz and Brian Rothwell, *The X&Y of Leadership*, 2000, The Industrial Society

Davis, Stan and Christopher Meyer, *Blur: The speed of change in the connected economy*, 1999, Grand Central Publishing

Eastwood, Mike, *The Charity Trustees Handbook*, 2010, Directory of Social Change

Forrest, Andrew and Patrick Tolfree, *Leaders: The learning curve of achievement*, 1992, The Industrial Society

Goleman, Daniel, *Emotional Intelligence: Why it can matter more than IQ*, 2005, Bantam Books

Hackman, Richard, *Leading Teams: Setting the stage for great performances*, 2002, Harvard Business School Press

Harris, John, *The Good Management Guide for the Voluntary Sector*, 2002, NCVO

Hawkins, Peter, *The Wise Fool's Guide to Leadership*, 2005, O-Books

Hind, Andrew, *The Governance and Management of Charities*, 1995, Voluntary Sector Press

Hudson, Mike, *Managing Without Profit*, 2017, Directory of Social Change

Hudson, Mike and Jacinta Ashworth, *Building Outstanding Leadership Teams*, 2014, Directory of Social Change

Johnson, Dr Spencer, *Who Moved My Cheese?*, 2002, Vermillion

Lawrie, Alan, *Business and Strategic Planning*, 2014, Directory of Social Change

Lawson, Ian, *Leaders for Tomorrow's Society*, 1999, The Industrial Society

Lewin, Roger and Birute Regime, *The Soul at Work*, 2000, Simon & Schuster

McMaster, Michael D., *The Intelligence Advantage: Organizing for complexity*, 1996, Butterworth-Heinemann

Maguire, Sheridan, *Core Coaching*, 2008, Directory of Social Change

Morris, Desmond, *The Human Zoo*, 1994, Vintage

Olivier, Richard, *Inspirational Leadership: Henry V and the Muse of Fire – Timeless insights from Shakespeare's greatest leader*, 2003, Spiro Press

Olivier, Richard and Nicholas Janni, *Peak Performance Presentations: How to present with passion and purpose*, 2004, Spiro Press

Pinker, Stephen, *How the Mind Works*, 2009, W. W. Norton & Company

Ranken, Wendy Blake, *The Good Employment Guide for the Voluntary Sector*, 2005, NCVO

Robinson, David, *Unconditional Leadership*, 2004, Community Links

Rothwell, Brian, *Team Building (Speed Read)*, 2009, Directory of Social Change

Rowntree, Derek, *Manager's Book of Checklists*, 2006, Pearson Education Ltd

Smith, Edwin Percy, *The Manager as a Leader (Notes for Managers)*, 1989, Industrial Society Press

Turner, David, *Liberating Leadership*, 1998, Industrial Society Press

Index